Here's what people are saying about
New Thinking, New Future by Sam Chand

Old thinking at best will keep you where you are in life and in all probability moves you back. My friend Sam Chand's book *New Thinking, New Future* reminds us that new places and spaces in leadership are awaiting us as soon as we embrace new thinking. You'll be challenged to grow, even as you help others do the same.

—*John C. Maxwell*
Best-Selling Author and Speaker

Sam Chand has dedicated his life to champion the success of others. Known as a "dream releaser," Sam is a leader of leaders who will constantly challenge and lift our mindsets, self-imposed limitations, and unexamined choices. Sam writes from the enormous wealth of his own experience with uncanny insight, good humor, and pragmatic advice. If you are hungry for a paradigm shift, to unlock unchartered dimensions of possibility for your life and leadership, *New Thinking, New Future* lays out a comprehensive "map and compass" to help you navigate the way.

—*Brian Houston*
Global Senior Pastor, Hillsong Church

Our world is changing faster than ever before in history. With new challenges and new opportunities emerging daily, we, as leaders, must work hard to change how we think, lead, and dream about what's possible. In his powerful book, *New Thinking, New Future*, Dr. Sam Chand will guide you through a series of crucial questions that won't just change how you think today, but will change how you impact lives in the future.

—*Craig Groeschel*
Founding Pastor, Life.Church
Host, *Craig Groeschel Leadership Podcast*

No one does this better than Sam Chand, and I can say that from our experience working with him in my own church. His reputation for helping companies find their way in the 21st century is exemplary and his integrity is beyond reproach. Whether you are a brand new company or ministry or, like us, you've been around for over thirty years, I can say with confidence that there is something transformational for you and your organization in his latest book, *New Thinking, New Future*.

—*Jentezen Franklin*
Senior Pastor, Free Chapel; *New York Times* Best-Selling Author

Great leaders have mastered the art of asking great questions, but legendary leaders like Sam Chand have mastered the art of questioning their own thinking. *New Thinking, New Future* is not just another leadership book; it's an introspective journey of self-discovery and self-awareness that could change everything for you and those you lead.

—*Steven Furtick*
Founder and Lead Pastor, Elevation Church

Just when I thought my friend, Sam Chand, had reached his pinnacle, he transcends to a new dimension. Sam has a masterful skill of asking piercing questions, which are better questions that lead to better answers and ultimately a better life! This is my kind of book! It will unlock a powerful, latent future within you!

—*Bishop Dale C. Bronner*
Author/Founder, Word of Faith Family Worship Cathedral

Sam Chand knows how our thought patterns color every decision we make—and *New Thinking, New Future* is proof he knows how to help us change them. With keys for dispelling negative, destructive thinking and cultivating a positive, life-giving perspective, Sam challenges and inspires us in ways both practical and profound. This book does something many books promise but few deliver—it changes your mind!

—*Chris Hodges*
Senior Pastor, Church of the Highlands
Author, *The Daniel Dilemma* and *What's Next?*

It is a sad truth that most businesses fail—and many quite quickly. The reason is most often not the lack of a noble vision, nor skills, nor detailed plans. Rather, it is the inability to cross the valley of execution—what Sam Chand calls the "muddy middle" between entrepreneurial dreams and marketplace victories. In the muddy middle, great plans are lost in the sea of ambiguity and confusion. In this book, *New Thinking, New Future*, Sam provides insights and advice for leaders navigating the challenges of building great businesses and organizations. These revelations will equip leaders entangled in traditional paradigms and frameworks with fresh ideas. As someone who has benefited from Sam's wisdom, your breakthrough could well be on the other side of reading this book.

—*Richard F. Chandler*
Founder and Chairman, Clermont Group

Dr. Sam Chand is one of the best-kept secrets in leadership development of this age. In his newest book, *New Thinking, New Future*, he gets real, up-close and personal—intentionally and at times uncomfortably so—to challenge us once again with essential questions of who we really are and who we really want to be. This is more than a book—it's a practical, groundbreaking, barrier-crushing leadership manual for newness in our personal leadership in ways we've not heard from him before.

—*Judah Smith*
Lead Pastor, Churchome

Change is on the horizon, but it will not come by accident—it will require intentionality by those who lead the way! As a voice of influence on the subject of leadership, my friend, Sam Chand, will help you shape your future by reshaping the way you think! *New Thinking New Future* will challenge you to examine your present patterns of thought and will reposition you to face the future with boldness.

—*John Bevere*
Best-Selling Author and Minister; Cofounder, Messenger International

If Michelangelo is correct, that "the true work of art is but a shadow of the divine perfection," Sam Chand casts a very long shadow. *New Thinking, New Future* is that master work and lifeline resource that could only be written from a lifetime of wisdom drawn directly from distinguished consulting contributions in the fields of business, church, and academy.

—*Leonard Sweet*
Best-Selling Author, *Bad Habits of Jesus*
Professor, Drew and George Fox Universities, Tabor College
Evangelical Seminary
Founder and Chief Contributor, preachthestory.com

I've known Dr. Sam Chand for years, and he's always had his finger on the pulse of the culture. His new book, *New Thinking, New Future*, takes that to an entirely new level. Sam answers eleven critically important questions about launching a new venture or leading an organization. Talk about accurate. I've been a media producer and consultant for many of the largest religious and nonprofit organizations in the country for nearly three decades, and these are exactly the questions leaders are asking. Get this book. It will save you more frustration than you could ever imagine.

—*Phil Cooke, Ph.D.*
Filmmaker; Writer; Media Consultant; and Founder, Cooke Media Group

Here is yet another practical leadership gem from a wise and seasoned leader, and a great tool to help leaders think differently, correctly, and effectively. The subject of our thinking is of critical importance to pastors and business leaders in a world more and more driven by emotion rather than by reason. Every leader would do well to include this well-set-out, clear book in his toolbox, as well as recommend it to their teams. What a great job Sam Chand has done on *New Thinking, New Future* as it resonates with the times we are living in where the thinking person is paid so much more than the doing person. I highly recommend it.

—*Andre Olivier*
Senior Pastor, Rivers Church, South Africa; Author and Speaker

If leaders are going to engage a rapidly changing culture with impact, they are going to have to be willing to change how they think, not just what they think. Sam Chand's thought-provoking, thought-changing book, *New Thinking, New Future*, is one every serious leader must read. Just the first chapter has already shaken up the way I think about how I think! Thanks, Sam, for such a great, groundbreaking work.

—*James Merritt*
Pastor and Former President, Southern Baptist Convention

New Thinking, New Future is not only relevant, but a must-read! Undeniably the right flight plan to the future!

—*Troy Korsgaden*
Insurance Carrier and Company Consultant

Throughout history, there have been introductions of "new things" that have changed everything. The discovery of electricity radically changed the way the world lives. The invention of the airplane revolutionized transportation. The creation of the computer transformed the way we do business. I believe the next "new thing" will bring about change within ourselves. In his groundbreaking book, *New Thinking, New Future*, Sam Chand masterfully outlines the path to a changed mindset and provides the catalyst for a brilliant future. I encourage you to read and reread this powerful book. It will change everything.

—*Dave Martin*
Your Success Coach; Author, *The 12 Traits of the Greats*

The secret to learning is to ask questions! Questions most often challenge our internal thoughts and set us on a course of discovery that enlarges our world. In his book, *New Thinking, New Future*, my long-time friend Dr. Sam Chand asks the questions that trigger a recalibration in our thinking, resulting in the possibility of greater outcomes. As a consultant and teacher, there is no one I've ever known who has more practical brilliance than Dr. Chand. I believe you will find this book practical, yet very challenging! I recommend you read it slowly, inhaling and exhaling often!

—*Tony Miller*
Bishop and Lead Pastor, The Gate Church
Founder and Visionary, Destiny Fellowship

God told me I was not to covet my neighbor's wife or my neighbor's animals, but the Bible is silent about coveting Sam Chand's perception. This guy sees things that others—including me—do not see. And Sam's latest book, *New Thinking, New Future*, is another example of the genius at work.

—*Anthony McLellan*
Chairman Emeritus, Australian Christian Lobby

A brilliant inward journey. *New Thinking, New Future* will facilitate a raw conversation with yourself about true success and impact. You will be forever changed.

—*Simon T. Bailey*
Breakthrough Strategist, Simon T. Bailey International, Inc.

Sam Chand has done it again. *New Thinking, New Future* is a thoughtful book on effective thinking. Leaders will find this book relevant, practical, and helpful. Sam summarizes what plagues us as leaders and furnishes sound solutions that we can actually practice. I recommend this book to any leader. Thank you, Sam.

—*Tim Elmore*
President, Growing Leaders

Dr. Sam Chand is a gift to the body of Christ and has a unique way of challenging leaders to think on a deeper level. The eleven questions in his new book, *New Thinking, New Future*, are questions every leader needs to wrestle with and answer. It is the answers to these questions that will propel your leadership to another level.

—*Daniel Floyd*
Founding Pastor, Life Point Church

He's done it again! When you think Sam Chand has written his best book, he comes along with even a better book. *New Thinking, New Future* is a glimpse into the mind of one of the top thinkers in the world. He will not only catch-you-up on thinking into today's language, but most of all, he will help you examine the ways you are currently thinking so you can become the leader you want to be.

—*Mike Robertson*
Lead Pastor, Visalia First

Sam Chand is an intentional leadership guru who gets the big picture! Leadership is contingent to the quality of our mental models, which bestow upon the leader the crucial ability to *see*. In a world where organizations are reactively impulsive, rather than reflectively intentional, this excellent leadership book is a must-read!

—*Edmund Chan*
Leadership Mentor, Covenant EFC Founder
Global Alliance of Intentional Disciple Making Churches

NEW
THINKING

NEW
FUTURE

SAMUEL R. CHAND

WHITAKER
HOUSE

New Thinking, New Future

Samuel R. Chand Consulting
950 Eagle's Landing Parkway Suite 295
Stockbridge, GA 30281
www.samchand.com

ISBN: 978-1-64123-217-3
eBook ISBN: 978-1-64123-218-0

Printed in the United States of America
© 2019 by Samuel R. Chand
All rights reserved.

Whitaker House
1030 Hunt Valley Circle
New Kensington, PA 15068
www.whitakerhouse.com

Library of Congress Cataloging-in-Publication Data
Names: Chand, Samuel R., author.
Title: New thinking, new future / Samuel R. Chand.
Description: New Kensington, PA : Whitaker House, 2019. |
Identifiers: LCCN 2018053111 (print) | LCCN 2018055902 (ebook) | ISBN 9781641232180 (e-book) | ISBN 9781641232173 (hardback)
Subjects: LCSH: Leadership. | Critical thinking. | BISAC: BUSINESS & ECONOMICS / Leadership. | BUSINESS & ECONOMICS / Motivational.
Classification: LCC HD57.7 (ebook) | LCC HD57.7 .C4677 2019 (print) | DDC 658.4/092019—dc23
LC record available at https://lccn.loc.gov/2018053111

1 2 3 4 5 6 7 8 9 10 11 **WH** 26 25 24 23 22 21 20 19

CONTENTS

1

The key to success is to risk thinking unconventional thoughts.
Convention is the enemy of progress.
If you go down just one corridor of thought you never
get to see what's in the rooms leading off it.
—Trevor Baylis

The way I think has changed over the years, and I've noticed the change even more in the recent past. For example, not long ago, I was asked to speak at a two-day event on the other side of the world. The people meeting with me told me about the history of the event, who had spoken in the past, and how many people were registered to attend. The offer was, by all measures, extraordinarily generous: first-class travel and accommodations, an ample honorarium, and an invitation for my wife, Brenda, to come along so we could enjoy a few extra days of vacation while we were there. The people who invited me couldn't have been more gracious. They asked me to look at my calendar and see if I was available.

In their minds, they had made me an offer I couldn't refuse. To them, our conversation was transactional: they wanted to secure a speaker for their planned event. They had done their homework, checking me out on social media and talking to people who had heard me speak. They were convinced I was the right person to speak at their next event.

A few years earlier, I would have looked at my calendar and if the dates were open, I would have instantly told them "yes." But in this season of my life, I wanted to think differently about the opportunity and ask a few more questions. I thanked them for their kind invitation, but my mind was a swirl of questions about issues beyond the prestige of speaking at their event, the money they would pay me, and the vacation Brenda and I would enjoy. I asked, "What do you expect to happen in the lives of the people who attend the event? What will be the long-term, existential impact on them?"

THINKING LONG-TERM

I could tell they assumed I would give a transactional response to their transactional offer; they were surprised when I asked additional questions. I sensed their frustration, so I explained:

"Let me tell you where I am in my life. I'm asking more questions about what I choose to do or not do, and I'm asking questions that are different than I've asked before. Here's what I want to know about my choices: Will every activity give me the opportunity to influence influencers? And can I be part of a leadership *journey* instead of just a leadership *event*? I'm not opposed to events, but I want to be assured that each event where I participate leads to a multiplied influence. I'm more interested in investing in long-term, existential impact than just isolated events. If I say 'yes' to the event, will we also commit to a relationship in which I work with your organization to build leaders after the event? I understand that the event gives me an inroad into the organization and credibility with the people who attend, so the event itself has value—but it has value to *me* only if I can participate with the organization to have a deeper, wider, longer impact. That's my focus today."

I thought I had explained myself very well, but one of them immediately began talking about the fee they were offering me. He had completely missed what I'd been telling them! His thought process was still transactional; so far, my existential reasoning hadn't made a dent. A few years before, the questions of the calendar and fees would have been at the top of my list, but now those questions were maybe fifth and sixth…while they were still one and two on this organization's list.

I realized then that we were thinking on two different wavelengths. They were trying to close a deal; I was interested in building a relationship. They wanted to finish our conversation by saying, "Done!" I wanted our conversation to begin by answering the question, "Where can we go together?"

Please don't misunderstand: I'm not insisting they were wrong and I was right. We were simply thinking on two different planes with two different sets of assumptions, two different goals, and two different processes to make decisions. Our questions were fundamentally different and to be honest, I had been exactly where they were only a short time before. They were seeking limited and specific goals, what some in the business world call key performing indices (KPI). I was operating according to the broader concept of objectives and key results (OKR). I'm much more interested in discuss-

ing the potential impact of any endeavor (i.e., the key results), which is almost always the result of meaningful relationships.

The way leaders think matters—it matters a lot. The problem is that we almost universally make a colossal subconscious assumption that the way we think is the only possible way to consider our situations. Our thought processes are so familiar, so ingrained, that we can't imag-

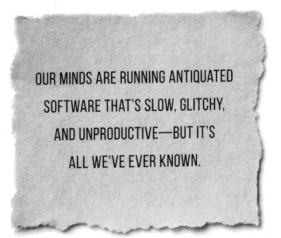

OUR MINDS ARE RUNNING ANTIQUATED SOFTWARE THAT'S SLOW, GLITCHY, AND UNPRODUCTIVE—BUT IT'S ALL WE'VE EVER KNOWN.

ine thinking a new way. It's like our minds are running antiquated software that's slow, glitchy, and unproductive—but it's all we've ever known. We need to upgrade the software in our heads! That's what this book is about.

IS IT POSSIBLE?

Is it even possible to change how we think? Yes, but it's not easy. Too often, our thinking patterns change when we encounter heartache, failure, and conflict, and the change may not be productive! Uncertainty makes us crave answers, but in times of difficulty, most people fill in the holes in their knowledge with fear and doubt instead of faith, reason, and hope.

To a large extent, our thought processes are shaped when we are young. I grew up in a very religious Christian environment in India, but it wasn't always positive. My parents were convinced their view of God and God's path for our lives was right and they were also sure anyone who disagreed with them was wrong. I bought into their perspective. We saw people as good or bad and teaching as right or wrong—no gray areas, no complexity, no rigorous discussions, just rigid certainty. Years after I came to America, I became the pastor of a similarly narrow, theologically rigid church. I felt right at home! Through a series of surprising events, I was asked to be the president of a Bible college. Suddenly, I led students who came from over fifty different Christian traditions, most of them unlike mine. During this time, I read an article that opened new doors to a world of new thinking. It said we need to realize there are three levels of commitment: to essentials, to convictions, and to preferences. I realized I had put virtually everything under the category of essentials and I expected everyone to agree with me. News flash: they didn't.

As the president, I also taught classes. One day after I had been think-ing about these levels of commitment, I walked into a class of about fifty students, representing, I assumed, at least thirty traditions. I asked them, "What are the core beliefs of the Christian faith?" As they voiced topics, I wrote them on the board. After only a few minutes, we had about thir-ty-five statements.

Then I turned and asked them, "If I put a gun to your head, which of these are you willing to die for?" The room became very quiet. Soon, a few brave students identified the few truths that were absolutely essential to their faith.

Like them, I realized a lot of the things that had seemed so important before were no longer things I'd die for. Few things are absolutely *essential* and worth our ultimate devotion and sacrifice. Some are *convictions* that we believe but won't die for. Most are simply *preferences*, like music genres, clothing styles, or the proper length of a pastor's sermon. (Well, that may rise to a conviction!)

The identification of essentials, convictions, and preferences is helpful in every aspect of life: at home, in business, in neighborhoods, and with friendships. Many heated conflicts can be avoided (or at least the temperature turned down below the boiling point) by recognizing people have the right to their own preferences. We also need to give them room for their convictions—and we can even love those who have different essentials, although we're sure ours will never change. This set of categories was very helpful for my students and it has been life-changing for me. I've learned to think differently. This simple but profound insight about how to think, perceive, and label people and ideas can radically change how we relate to virtually everyone we know. We will be more open to others' ideas, less defensive about at least some of our own, and more willing to appreciate different perspectives. What kind of difference would this make on a staff team or an executive team in goal-setting and planning? In a marriage and our relationships with our children? It makes a world of difference—and it all happens when we learn a different way to think.

> THE IDENTIFICATION OF ESSENTIALS, CONVICTIONS, AND PREFERENCES IS HELPFUL IN EVERY ASPECT OF LIFE: AT HOME, IN BUSINESS, IN NEIGHBORHOODS, AND WITH FRIENDSHIPS.

The processes and contents of our thoughts determine everything: optimism or pessimism, persistence or apathy, security or uncertainty, care or recklessness—and seeing people as assets or viewing them as threats. Developmental psychologists tell us our perceptions are formed in the first years of life. Children are sponges, instinctively absorbing the emotions, values, and beliefs of those around them. These concepts are seldom *taught* by the adults in their lives, but they are *caught* like we catch viruses in the air we breathe or the things we touch. Some of us, to be sure, have caught viruses of racism, pride, shame, and xenophobia. Virtually all of us have absorbed values that are important to our families, but upon closer inspection, aren't really important at all.

For instance, Brenda and I grew up on different continents, but our families seldom, if ever, served fish. To this day, Brenda never eats fish and I eat it only a couple of times a year. We have been married for almost forty years and we've never cooked a piece of fish in our home. Neither of us read a scholarly article and decided to avoid fish. Our thoughts about it are the product of the (mostly unspoken) messages in our homes when we were children. Those messages still shape our decisions today. Our essentials, convictions, and preferences have been firmly implanted by those who shaped our early environments.

These early perceptions and thinking patterns are deeply ingrained in us, so it requires considerable wisdom and effort to change them. Most of us have never tried to step out of ourselves to analyze how we think; we just use the same old software that was downloaded many years before.

ASKING THE WRONG QUESTION

Almost universally, leaders ask the wrong question. They assume their thinking is good, right, and productive, so they jump to, "What am I going to *do* about this?" Instead, perhaps they should start a step earlier and ask, "How should I *think* about this?"

What prompts us to evaluate how we think? Sometimes, a friend or mentor prods us to see a situation from a different angle that requires us to think in a different way. But more often, a cataclysmic event shatters our closely-held assumptions about the way life should work and we're forced to reframe what we believe, who we trust, and how we think. If you have a choice, go with the first option: the mentor instead of the catastrophe! Those who are closest to us are often the first to notice that our thinking needs some remediation.

When I was a child, my parents only knew one way to discipline us. They had never heard of "time out"; they spanked us for every offense. Not surprisingly, when our girls were little, I followed my parents' example. One day after I'd spanked Rachel, Brenda walked into the room as Rachel ran out crying. Looking at me with a powerful blend of exasperation and hope, Brenda said, "Sam, have you noticed that the only way you know to discipline the girls is to spank them?"

It was like she was asking if I knew water is wet. I had no idea why she would ask the question. Thankfully, I had the good sense to respond,

"I'm not at all sure what you're trying to say. Would you explain what you mean?" This began an eye-opening conversation about my childhood and my very narrow range of parenting skills, especially regarding discipline. It opened a door to a new way to think and respond to my daughters. The change was as dramatic as it was welcome. Everyone was happy Brenda had the courage to ask me a hard question.

We have powerful but largely unevaluated thinking patterns about a host of important elements of our lives: food, time, sex, possessions, privacy, savings, spending, giving, debt, and many others. Twice in the past, Brenda and I became overextended with credit card debt. Like most couples, it was easy to get into trouble and very hard to get out of it, but we did. Some people told us the problem was the credit cards, but I knew they weren't the culprit. The real problem was human, not plastic. We got out of debt, but we still use credit cards. We pay them off every month, so we're known as nonrevolvers—a moniker I'm proud to earn. If we had blamed the cards for our trouble, I'm not sure we would have learned important lessons about how to think about limits on spending.

HIDDEN BLOCKAGES

My friend Edmund Chan has observed that most of us, even the most successful among us, have a swirl of negative thoughts that affect how we think, what we feel, what we decide, and how we relate to the people around us. If these are left unresolved, they keep us prisoners of defective and destructive thinking patterns.[1] These include:

PRIMAL WOUNDS OF THE HEART: "I HURT"

If we're alive, we've been hurt. We've been ignored, unfairly criticized or blamed, intimidated, used, and betrayed...countless times. When these hurts remain unhealed, ungrieved, and unforgiven, we erect walls to prevent anyone from hurting us again. We may also react defensively and angrily to the smallest slight because it reminds us of the greater hurt that still poisons our hearts. When old hurts aren't healed, we try to avoid any new wounds, but we remain fragile, vulnerable, and easily hurt again. Some try to be exceedingly sweet so no one will hurt them; others try to

---

1. Adapted from *Growing Deep in God* by Edmund Chan (Singapore: Covenant Evangelical Free Church, 2008).

intimidate to keep people away or dominate them; and many become passive-aggressive, trying to appear innocent while they stick a knife of revenge in those who seem to threaten them.

CYNICISM OF THE MIND: "I DOUBT"

A collection of small wounds *erodes* trust, but even a single major betrayal *shatters* trust. To protect ourselves, we learn to doubt others' motives and be suspicious of their actions. But our cynicism doesn't stop with our perception of others; many of us live with severe self-doubt, questioning every motive, every decision, and harshly blaming ourselves for any perceived failure. Cynicism causes us to be defensive around others and brutal to ourselves. It has a hard edge of suspicion; it wants to find fault and delights in condemnation. Healthy skepticism, on the other hand, is simply due diligence; it asks good questions and welcomes honest answers.

PARALYSIS OF THE WILL: "I CAN'T"

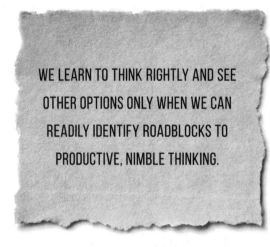

WE LEARN TO THINK RIGHTLY AND SEE OTHER OPTIONS ONLY WHEN WE CAN READILY IDENTIFY ROADBLOCKS TO PRODUCTIVE, NIMBLE THINKING.

Unhealed wounds and a cynical mind sometimes produce a compelling demand to be on top, to win at all cost, but more often, it results in the opposite effect: hopelessness and passivity. We come up with plenty of excuses—"I'm too old." "I'm too young." "I'm not educated enough." "I don't have what it takes." If people dwell on these excuses long enough, perception becomes reality: hopelessness pervades their thinking and they feel completely helpless. Opportunities come and go because the person doesn't have enough confidence to even try.

SIX COMMON BARRIERS

We learn by clearly identifying contrasts: we choose *this* instead of *that*; we believe *this* concept because *that* one doesn't ring true. We learn to think rightly only when we can readily identify the roadblocks to productive, nimble thinking. Only then can we see other options. I want to point out six common barriers to critical thinking:

1. SOCIAL CONDITIONING

As we've seen, our thoughts, beliefs, values, and decisions are, to a great degree, a product of our social environment. All of us are socially conditioned; it's unavoidable. We can be locked into our perceptions based on race, religion, politics, nationality, and every other conceivable factor, down to the sports team we cheer for...and the ones we can't stand.

The messages we internalized inflame our beliefs and limit our choices. We hold fast to particular ideas and prejudices even when we find ample evidence against them. We listen to "experts" who confirm our biases and we disregard those who have an opposing view. We can't imagine living in certain neighborhoods, driving particular cars, having a wider range of friends, or marrying a specific kind of person. I'm quite sure Brenda's parents and friends were stunned when she told them she wanted to marry a guy from India!

2. INSTANT JUDGMENT

Based on our social conditioning and past experiences, we prejudge people and ideas, eliminating them from careful consideration, shutting off conversation, perceiving their values as defective, and seeing them as enemies of all we hold right and good.

I've noticed that the longer a leader serves in an organization, the greater the propensity for pessimism. Old hurts haven't quite healed, hard words aren't forgotten, and the memory of past opposition still lingers. All become a recipe for instantly assuming any question, even an honest, good-hearted one, represents an attack on the leader's position and character.

The answer isn't to be naïve. Good leaders have a blend of healthy skepticism and openness to new ideas. President Ronald Reagan famously stated his policy about the Soviet Union: "Trust but verify."

3. EGOCENTRIC

In a self-absorbed, unreflective, defensive mind, people assume their thinking is always right and others are always wrong. This, of course, predisposes them to instant judgments and they use power plays to domi-nate and intimidate those who might disagree.

To counter this tendency in my life, I've learned to walk into a meeting and say, "I have a great idea, but I need you to make it even better." This simple statement tells the people on our team that I'm a leader who initi-ates creative new plans, but it also tells them I value each one of them and welcome their input.

4. ALWAYS CERTAIN

Some people are so insecure that they hide behind the protective walls of absolute certainty. They feel uncomfortable with complexity and they refuse to live with ambiguity. They don't want to think abstractly; they insist on concrete solutions, so every question must have a definite and irrefutable answer. They see people as all good or all bad, totally loyal or completely suspect, and they are either fully behind an idea, candidate, or organization, or they fiercely oppose them.

When I was a college president, staff at different levels often asked me to help them solve problems. I learned to listen carefully and then ask them to come back with three possible solutions. If I had asked them for only two, they would probably come with one good solution and one that was obviously inferior. Asking them for three required them to get out of binary thinking and be more complex and thorough. Sometimes, I really stretched them by asking for four or five possible solutions.

5. BLINDLY LOYAL

Some people don't want to think for themselves, so they believe what-ever those in authority tell them. After all, they surmise, those people got to the top for a reason. They may exhibit blind loyalty to a person, a group, or an institution, and they don't want to listen if someone has even a mildly critical view of this authority. Quite often, this response is the product of being raised by parents who used more limits than love and more demands than kindness with their children.

I'm certainly not saying the problem is always the leader's fault for exercising authority. Leaders must lead. They must wield authority and influence to be effective. The problem here is in the minds of the followers, those who aren't secure enough to be objective and ask good questions.

Today, leaders need to understand that different groups of people may mean very different things by their questions. Millennial leaders feel very comfortable with other people in the organization asking, "Why?" These leaders know the person is genuinely searching for answers. But Boomer leaders may hear the same question and interpret it as a challenge to their authority, responding defensively and harming the relationship. These older leaders too often interpret blind loyalty as a positive character trait. It's not. It kills creativity.

6. GO ALONG TO GET ALONG

Some people are conflict-avoidant, so they don't question people who have different opinions, even if they don't agree. This lack of mental involvement almost completely shuts down innovation. These people aren't blindly loyal. They see the flaws in their leaders and members of their teams, but they're not willing to engage in meaningful conversation to change minds or invest their best efforts in achieving the organization's objectives.

BREAKING THROUGH BARRIERS

When we can identify these barriers in others, we can help them make better choices, find freedom, and serve with passion and creativity. When we identify the barriers in ourselves, we uncover choices that lead to the most challenging and rewarding paths of our lives. We suddenly have more options, more intellectual energy, and more innovative solutions than ever before.

OUT OF THE BOX

I've noticed that the best leaders use three kinds of thinking: strategic, genius, and oblique. Throughout most organizations, people in different roles often use *strategic* thinking. Their goal is to accomplish a task, so they think through the basic questions to make sure every base is covered. They ask questions about *who*, *what*, *when*, *where*, and *how*. They may or may not ask *why* because they assume others have already thought through that question.

GENIUS THINKING IS DIFFERENT

Genius thinking asks, "What if…?" These leaders begin to contemplate their options even before they start crafting any kind of formal plan. They know they have some resources in hand and they know how to find other resources. Other resources may be out of reach, but they don't limit their vision to the ones they can readily identify. They dream, they imagine, and they envision possibilities. When they don't have enough resources, they're even more resourceful. Some might ask, "Which is better, strategic thinking or genius thinking?" The answer is "both." Like two wings of an airplane, leaders need both kinds to thrive.

As organizations grow larger and more complex, leaders need to engage in *oblique* thinking. By the time a challenge or opportunity reaches their desks, these issues are far beyond strategic thinking and they often don't have clear answers even genius thinking is looking for. At this point, there's no right or wrong, no black or white; there are multiple answers and all of them have promised benefits and potential risks. The answers to these questions often are both/and rather than either/or.

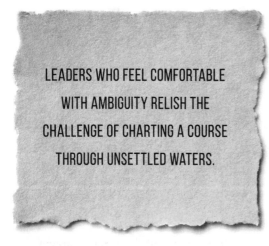

LEADERS WHO FEEL COMFORTABLE WITH AMBIGUITY RELISH THE CHALLENGE OF CHARTING A COURSE THROUGH UNSETTLED WATERS.

Some leaders are stuck in strategic thinking and lack creativity. They're good managers, but they seldom inspire people around them and their organizations usually remain a modest size. Genius thinkers are looking outside the box, but they're still expecting to find clear paths forward. Their organizations grow because they think in terms of possibilities, not limits.

A few leaders feel comfortable with ambiguity. They don't insist on guaranteed outcomes for their biggest decisions. In fact, they relish the challenge of charting a course through unsettled waters. The people closest to them often become genius thinkers and a few might even learn to think obliquely.

What kind of thinker are you? Press, stretch, and grow to become a genius thinker, and perhaps even learn to think obliquely.[2]

PRACTICAL PAYOFFS

The questions I'll address in this book peel back the layers of our assumptions and challenge us to think more deeply, more clearly, and more productively than ever before. We'll look at the fundamental topics all leaders instinctively address, including security, location, ownership, team, growth, and benchmarks of success. It's not easy to step out of ourselves to think about thinking, but it's essential—and the payoffs are enormous. Let me list a few:

YOU'LL WELCOME NEW IDEAS

Other people see things from a different perspective. That doesn't make them wrong and it doesn't make them right. It only means they may have something to offer that we haven't considered before. As our defenses go down, new ideas are no longer seen as a threat. We can live with nuances and we aren't thrown off guard by complexity. A new world of options opens to us.

YOU'LL BE MORE APPROACHABLE

The corollary to welcoming new ideas is that the people with those ideas feel welcomed. We value their experiences, their perspectives, and their suggestions. They may have a different way of saying the same thing, but their way may work better with part of your audience, so you learn from them. Or they may have diametrically different views, even about the essentials of your life and faith, but you're secure enough to engage in meaningful dialogue without demanding or intimidating. When we talk to people who have a different perspective, we don't react. Instead, we say those magical words, "Tell me more about that." This simple statement works wonders.

When we're approachable, others sense it. They pick it up by our non-verbal cues: our gestures, the look in our eyes, our tone of voice, and our body language. They feel comfortable being themselves in our presence.

---

2. Three kinds of thinking is adapted from "Creative Leadership," *Futuring* (Highland Park, IL: Mall Publishing, 2002, 123–128.

When we need directions and there are five people standing on the corner, we look for the person whose appearance communicates, "You can ask me. I'll be glad to help." When we're shopping, we're drawn to the sales clerk who has open gestures and a ready smile, not the intense one who has pursed lips and a furrowed brow. One is happy to show us the shoes we're looking for; the other makes us feel we're an inconvenient distraction.

YOU'LL BE MORE PATIENT WITH YOURSELF

Many leaders are in a hurry. They have a vision and they're desperately trying to move heaven and earth to fulfill their dream. They aren't very patient with others who aren't running as fast as they are and they aren't patient with themselves. Great leaders realize the best ideas, the best products, and the best results come from a process, a process that is stunted by hurrying. Yes, they have big plans. Yes, they have a lot to do. But the most important aspects of leadership—thinking and planning—require ideas to marinate until they are ready for the oven.

I was born impatient. Now is too late! Everything should have happened yesterday! But over the years, I've learned to value the process of starting with good ideas, thinking about them, and getting others to think about them, until they become great ideas.

Brenda used to frustrate me with her commitment to process. I wondered how a simple question could inspire so much thought. Her silence was deafening. Over the years, she has learned to say, "I'm thinking." And I've learned to respond, "I know."

YOU'LL COMMUNICATE MORE CLEARLY

As leaders ask more questions and listen more carefully, they understand their people far better. Their message then goes beyond facts to connect with the hopes and fears that have surfaced in the conversations. These leaders now understand not only what people need to do, but how they feel, what they believe, and how they dream. When leaders connect with people on that level, they accelerate motivation and engagement.

The best communicators "read the room" to notice how their message is being heard. Even before that, they anticipate responses so they can say,

"Some of you are thinking…" or "Some of you are feeling…" and "Some of you have these concerns…."

YOU'LL MAKE BETTER DECISIONS

When we think more expansively, we consider more options, involve more people, develop a better grid to sort out ideas, and come out with better decisions for ourselves and those around us.

My thinking about decisions has changed over the years. I used to instantly ask, "Can I do this?" then "How much will it cost?" I've learned to begin with the question, "Who do I need?"

For instance, I was asked to help in the reorganization of a major, nationwide company. The first question I asked myself was, "Who do I need on my team to help these leaders pull off the best possible reorganization?" Better questions lead to better results.

YOUR EXPECTATIONS

Every executive is hired for one primary purpose: to make the hardest decisions in the organization. Whether it's the president of the United States, the CEO of a company, or the pastor of a church, each one is hired to make decisions that will solve seemingly intractable problems and propel the organization forward. Others give input and provide data, but the executive must make the final decisions. Better decisions,

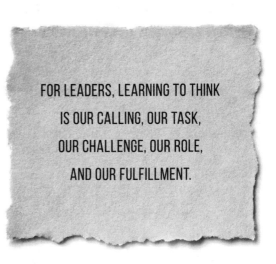

FOR LEADERS, LEARNING TO THINK IS OUR CALLING, OUR TASK, OUR CHALLENGE, OUR ROLE, AND OUR FULFILLMENT.

though, don't come out of thin air and they aren't the product of chance. They are the result of high-level thinking processes, which then can be articulated as viable options so the best choice can be made. Only then will the team spring into action, implementing plans, seeing tangible results, and fulfilling the organization's destiny.

Learning to think, then, isn't optional for leaders. It's our calling, our task, our challenge, our role, and our fulfillment. You can choose your thoughts as carefully as you choose what you wear. Explore your thought processes and challenge your assumptions. Cultivate new ways to think about old problems and new opportunities. Be brave enough to ask yourself hard questions and be a leader who excels at asking others great questions. Pick up new ways to think. Dress your mind on purpose!

If you learn to think better, you'll be a better leader. I guarantee it. Become an expert at asking penetrating questions. If no one ever says to you, "Nobody has ever asked me that question," you need to learn to go deeper. If you become a person who thinks more clearly, expansively, and nimbly, you'll also be a better leader, speaker, spouse, parent, and friend.

Let me be very practical with you now. Pastor Craig Groeschel is a phenomenal leader. At a conference, he gave a talk on "Busting Barriers with Mindset Changes." He addressed the need to think differently about a range of important topics, including organizational culture, programming, purpose, and limitations. His first recommendation to implement these principles was, "Find someone one or two steps ahead of you and learn how they think. Most want to learn what they do—not what they think."[3] That's my advice to you: If you want to be a better leader, invest time and energy in being a better thinker. But realize you'll make much more progress if you have a coach, a mentor, or a wise friend who is farther along than you are. Lean on this person, be open to suggestions, and realize that being uncomfortable with progress is entirely normal.

In the next chapters, I'll ask ten more crucial questions. I've asked myself these questions, and they've helped me grow. I trust they'll do the same thing for you.

At the end of each chapter, you'll also find some questions to stimulate your thinking and focus your application. Use these for personal reflection and discussions with your coach. You may also want to use them as a guide for group discussions with your team.

---

3. Cited by Will Mancini, "Groeschel on Thinking Different: Culture, Programming & Mission," https://www.willmancini.com/blog/groeschel-on-thinking-different-culture-programming-mission.

THINK ABOUT IT...

1. Do you agree or disagree with the point that virtually all of us make colossal assumptions as the basis of our thinking? Explain your answer.

2. How does it help to differentiate between essentials, convictions, and preferences? How does making virtually everything an essential inevitably lead to conflict?

3. Why are messages we absorbed in our childhood so ingrained and hard to change?

4. Look at the three negative assumptions: "I hurt," "I doubt," and "I can't." Which of these has the biggest impact on your thinking and your life? Describe the impact it has made.

5. Which of the payoffs of better thinking is most attractive to you? Explain your answer.

6. How would it help you think more deeply and clearly if you have a mentor who is one or two steps ahead of you in this pursuit? Who might be this person in your life?

7. Why are you reading this book? What do you hope to get out of it?

2

HOW WILL I KNOW I'M SUCCESSFUL?
THE QUESTION OF BENCHMARKS

Like success, failure is many things to many people.
With positive mental attitude, failure is a learning experience,
a rung on the ladder, and a plateau at which to get your
thoughts in order to prepare to try again.
—W. Clement Stone

The Appalachian Trail offers one of the most popular and challenging hikes in America. Its 2,187 miles traverse the eastern United States from Springer Mountain in Georgia to Mt. Katahdin in Maine. Along the way, the U.S. Forest Service has built two hundred and fifty sites with permanent shelters, but hikers spend most nights in tents. Every year, more than two thousand people start the trek and a few hundred make it from one end to the other. If you ask a hiker on the north side of Springer Mountain how he defines "success," he might give any of several answers. He might say, "When I'm standing on the top of Katahdin in a few months," or he might tell you, "I hope to make a hundred miles by the end of this week," or he may shrug and smile, "If I get to the first campsite by sundown, I'll be happy."

The vast majority of people who hike the Appalachian Trail have limited goals. They look at their official maps and find a nice ten-mile hike for a day or maybe twenty-five miles for a three-day weekend. The ones who have the highest goal of trudging the entire length of the trail are called "thru-hikers." Some of them have serious self-doubts at the beginning, but they take that first step. Far more are plagued with the prospect of having to stop because they sprain an ankle, get sick, find out they're needed at home, or discover the exhaustion of hiking outweighs the romance of the journey they hoped they'd find.

In her personal reflections on the glories and difficulties of hiking "the AT," Maggie Wallace remarks that the worry of not finishing can rob people of the joy of the journey. She writes:

> We were so wrapped up in the question, "What if I don't make it?" that we were almost afraid to have fun. The AT isn't your job, and no one can say anything to change that.
>
> There's a petty side to human nature that seeks to tear down strong people because we interpret their success as an offense to our own inadequacy. The words of the people who succumb to this have no bearing on you, so don't let anyone's arbitrary benchmarks determine your actions. It doesn't matter if you begin the trail out of shape or without hiking experience. You're the only person who can say whether or not you're going to finish.
>
> If you believed what people said, you wouldn't be standing on Springer.[4]

The same principle is true in every pursuit in our lives. Yes, we have an ultimate goal, but we make more progress when we enjoy each step of the journey instead of worrying about events and outcomes too far in the future. We need to celebrate the incremental benchmarks of success so we have encouragement to keep going toward the ultimate success.

---

4. "11 things I wish I'd known before hiking the Appalachian Trail," Maggie Wallace, Matador Network, July 25, 2014, https://matadornetwork.com/sports/11-things-wish-knew-hiking-appalachian-trail.

LIFE'S LITTLE MOMENTS

My friend Daniel Floyd, pastor of Lifepoint Church in Fredericksburg, Virginia, has some insightful observations about the often unnoticed but vitally important steps forward. He observes that no one pays much attention to a first date, but the wedding is a big celebration. No one stands and applauds as we spend hours studying, but they come to our graduation ceremony. Very few

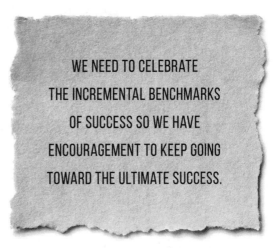

WE NEED TO CELEBRATE THE INCREMENTAL BENCHMARKS OF SUCCESS SO WE HAVE ENCOURAGEMENT TO KEEP GOING TOWARD THE ULTIMATE SUCCESS.

people pat us on the back when we save some of our income, but everybody comes to the open house when we have enough money for a down payment on a new home.

Leaders "can think life is all about the milestones, the big moments, but it's really about the little moments that eventually lead us to the big moments," Daniel says. "To get there requires commitment to put forth the effort to go to the next level. It's the willingness to do whatever it takes to be a better leader and a better person, and to do those things when no one is applauding."

Daniel points to God's directions to the children of Israel as they prepared to enter the Promised Land. (See Exodus 23.) God said He would lead them to drive out the inhabitants of Canaan step by step and area by area. Each movement forward required a new surge of commitment and effort. The slow, steady pace of success was a form of God's grace to them. As God explained to Moses:

> *But I will not drive them out in a single year, because the land would become desolate and the wild animals too numerous for you. Little by little I will drive them out before you, until you have increased enough to take possession of the land.* (Exodus 23:29–30)

God was saying the Israelites couldn't handle it if He gave them too much too soon. For the children of Israel and for us, the dedication we muster and the wisdom we gain on the journey are the ways God prepares us for the next steps we take.[5]

The Bible offers us lessons that are still applicable to life today.

THREE CRUCIAL QUESTIONS

In my conversations with leaders, I've learned to ask them three questions: about their dream, their process, and their measuring stick.

1. WHERE IS "THERE"?

I've found that many leaders have moving goalposts. Those in business may tell me about projected revenues in one conversation, but a few months later, they talk more about opening stores in new locations. Pastors often tell me they want their churches to grow, but the numbers they throw out often seem like they were pulled out of a hat. I'm not trying to be critical of the dreams of leaders, but sooner or later (preferably sooner), dreams need to take on a more concrete form. If leaders can't define their ultimate aim, they'll be frustrated, and their communication with others will be somewhat confusing. It takes work to think carefully and deeply about where "there" is in a leader's dreams, but it's essential so everyone is clear about where the organization is going.

2. HOW WILL YOU KNOW YOU'RE THERE?

Leaders often talk about "more"—more revenues, stores, products, customers, or even people being developed as rising leaders. All of those are good, but what does "more" mean? Everything important in life has a number: Social Security, blood pressure, heart rate, homes and apartments, vehicle identification numbers on cars, and on and on. The highest and best goal of an organization may include numbers, but it's more than how many dollars, sites, and noses. Numbers aren't wrong, but they aren't enough. It's a question of impact: what difference will it make to the community and everyone involved for the benchmarks to be achieved?

---

5. "Starting Small and Finishing Strong," Daniel Floyd, Senior Pastor of Lifepoint Church, Tuesdays with Sam Chand, http://tuesdayswithsamchand.com.

3. WHAT ARE THE INTERMEDIATE BENCHMARKS OF PROGRESS?

These benchmarks may be different than one might expect. For instance, when a business leader has a goal of developing his staff so the company can expand on the shoulders of men and women who share his vision, he can look for those who take ideas in staff meetings and develop them into something more than he expected. These people are going above and beyond.

A benchmark of progress isn't having names in each slot on the organizational chart. Real progress is shown when there are more people eager and prepared for the next position up the ladder than the positions available. That's the benchmark we should be looking for! Another benchmark may be more employees who are equipped, engaged, and enthused about volunteering in the community, or deciding to further their education. This commitment says something about the organization's culture and it says something about the leader.

For churches, other benchmarks include stronger marriages (revealed by fewer separations and divorces), more people enrolling in higher education, a lower unemployment rate among parishioners, more community outreach programs of compassion for "the least of these," and being a respected part of the community, which is demonstrated by city officials, the police and fire departments, schools, and private agencies seeing the pastor and the church as a trusted resource. In other words, if the local police department needs help raising money for body cameras, do they turn to your church for assistance? If the fire department wants to canvass an area to provide information or supplies, will they call on your church to help? If the mayor is wrestling with conflict in a part of the city, does she turn to you and your church to help lower the tension and resolve the problem? When catastrophes like hurricanes, tornadoes, or fires devastate homes and families, can the leaders of the city count on your church? These and many other scenarios are signs that the church is having a profound impact.

THE MUDDY MIDDLE

Many leaders have observed that the hardest part of the journey to reach their dreams isn't the beginning or the end. The beginning is full of energy, hope, and enthusiasm; the end is a great celebration, sometimes coupled with exhaustion. The middle is the problem. It's the time when enthusiasm has waned and difficulties have surfaced. People—sometimes leaders—wonder if they're on the right path, if they'll make it, and if it's worth all the trouble. A tremendous amount of effort and money has already been expended, but the new site hasn't opened, the new product is still in development, the new software still has bugs in it, the money hasn't all been raised, and people are wondering if the leader is doing anything at all. At the beginning, everyone was motivated; at the end, there will be a party; but in the middle, skilled leaders know they continually need to inject fresh motivation because it has atrophied and they need to celebrate each incremental step so people don't lose focus.

> THE MIDDLE OF THE JOURNEY IS WHEN ENTHUSIASM HAS WANED AND DIFFICULTIES HAVE SURFACED.

Each major project or product—or perhaps a goal to expand to X number of additional stores or restaurants—has a timeline with an exciting beginning, an ambiguous middle, and a celebratory completion. As leaders, we are wise to set clear and attainable intermediate benchmarks that call for the best from every person. We need to work especially hard in the middle of a project to maintain momentum.

We can also apply this principle to personal development for ourselves and those who report to us. Leaders are better at setting goals than most people, so they have a leg up already. But all of us are very human and we're subject to the same pattern of starting strong, getting bogged down in the middle, and being tempted to give up before we reach our goal. We need to keep injecting motivation and celebrations for incremental progress as we move forward with our finances, our weight, our knowledge of important subjects, our marriages, our relationships with our kids, and every other significant aspect of our lives. Watch for a slip of momentum between the enthusiastic beginning and reaching the goal!

The ambiguous middle can be a dangerous place. If we don't pay attention, discouragement can rob us of enthusiasm, and then apathy and confusion will creep into our leadership style and our organizations—we'll lose our cutting edge. Most failing businesses and organizations begin dying about two years before there are obvious signs of decline. Like a tree with fungus in its roots, what's visible may continue to look healthy even while disease is killing it. Strong, vibrant organizations are led by people who regularly prune away dead or dying parts, fertilize often to stimulate growth, and continually add the water of vision and encouragement. They create a culture that can withstand cycles of ups and downs, expand and deepen the leadership pipeline, and introduce fresh enthusiasm through a renewed vision of the future.

TRUST YOUR GUT

Some of us are highly intuitive; some are more analytical. In fact, the most important decisions in our lives are led by our "gut," not our heads: who we marry, our choice of a career, the house we buy or rent, the car we drive, the church we attend, the doctor we visit, the vacations we take, and the restaurants we frequent. These choices have a modicum of reasoning attached, but we make these decisions largely by what we feel, by intuition. The person we ask to give the eulogy at our funeral may be our best friend, who knows our heart, rather than the church pastor. The friend may not be as articulate, but we're convinced they will represent us well.

Think back on a time when you weighed the pros and cons of an important decision. Something inside may have screamed, "No! Don't do it!" but your reasoning prompted you to go ahead—and later you realized your gut was right. Some people insist that we shouldn't go by our feelings, but our feelings and intuition are part of our God-given nature. We certainly shouldn't depend on our feelings alone, but they are more important—and more accurate—than most people believe.

People in your community make decisions about your business or organization based largely on their feelings. In an article titled, "Trust Your Feelings, Now More Than Ever," Robert Safian, editor of *Fast Company*, writes:

Business isn't always about numbers. Actually, it rarely is. It's about people and emotion. What about the dollars? The cash flow? The share price? Don't kid yourself. Those are the by-products, the results. Anyone who is truly sophisticated about business recognizes this essential truth.

Safian describes some colossal failures when companies didn't connect emotionally with their customers and he lists some stunning successes when they went beyond reason to provide products and services to meet real needs in underserviced parts of the community. He concludes:

> What makes "brand" so important? It describes the emotional connection that consumers, employees, partners, regulators, and everyone else has with an organization. Once upon a time, a brand could be constructed independently of a product, of the working conditions at facilities, of environmental and cultural impact. Those days are over. Today, a brand stands for something, organically, reflected in social media engagement and societal dialogue. Nothing is insulated or off limits—even politics and religion. The burden on business leaders has grown, and so has the opportunity.[6]

When we're in the middle of the journey, our minds may tell us to bail out, but our gut reminds us that it's worth it. And throughout the journey, we need to remember that we're not the only ones who depend on our feelings to give us signals of meaning and direction. The people on our teams, our customers and clients, our volunteers, and the people in our communities make their decisions based on their feelings, too. We're wise to connect *our* purpose and our passion to *their* purpose and passion.

ORGANIZATIONAL CONGRUENCE

The lack of organizational congruence is another type of mud, but it can be avoided by better thinking, planning, and communicating. Congruence is the alignment of the leader's vision and values with the vision and values of the board, the leadership team, and the entire organization. When it's present, every activity—planning, budgeting, personnel selection and

---

6. "Trust Your Feelings, Now More Than Ever," Robert Safian, *Fast Company*, August 14, 2017, https://www.fastcompany.com/40437744/trust-your-feelings-now-more-than-ever.

training, and implementation of projects, products and services—moves together to fulfill the stated objectives. When this is happening, people know where "there" is, they know what kind of impact getting "there" will accomplish, and they have clear intermediate benchmarks that keep them motivated during the middle period of the journey.

Too often, I've sensed or seen divergent agendas in organizations. I meet with the leader and I hear a clear, compelling vision of where the organization is meant to go, but when I meet with board members, people on the executive team, or staff, I get a slightly different picture—or occasionally, a radically different picture. In these cases, it's easy to figure out why people are confused and why conflict exists. People are rowing in different directions!

Congruence doesn't mean everybody always agrees and there's no room for creative thought. The healthy give and take of ideas is one of the most important corporate values. The executive team, the staff and workers, and the volunteers all need to give their best thinking and their best suggestions. When a decision is made, they need to give their best efforts to accomplish the goal. Success will be elusive, and life will be a grind, if the leader and the rest of the organization aren't on the same page.

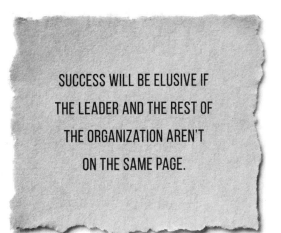

SUCCESS WILL BE ELUSIVE IF THE LEADER AND THE REST OF THE ORGANIZATION AREN'T ON THE SAME PAGE.

Creativity is one of the most important signs of a healthy organization, but innovative ideas, processes, and products need to be evaluated to see if they extend the vision and values of the organization or if they take it slightly off course. Gifted, wise leaders know they can't and shouldn't implement every great idea. Some are congruent, but some aren't. In every conversation about the future, the topic of organizational congruence needs to be present, at least in the leader's thinking and often in the middle of the conversation with the team. When we're thinking correctly, we see the inevitable tradeoffs for every decision. When we launch a new endeavor, we almost always need to lay another one aside.

In an article titled "The Upside of a Tradeoff," Basecamp co-founder Jason Fried comments:

> By forcing a tradeoff on every new "yes," you corner yourself into considering the value of something. And only once you value a thing accordingly can you make a better decision about what is worth pursuing. It requires you to reconsider: Is this still worth doing? Would we be better off doing something else? That's a healthy exercise from time to time. The true test of how bad you want something is whether you're willing to give up something else to make room.[7]

Every "yes" is pregnant with a "no." Every choice has a cost. Count the costs of a "yes" and a "no."

Vision and values must be constantly communicated. If not, the attention of people will drift toward what is tangible and easily measurable: the numbers. The finest corporate leaders continually point their people to a bigger vision, higher goals, and more important values:

+ At the end of the day, you want to be profitable, but that's not the meaning of life. —Daniel Lamarre, Cirque du Soleil

+ To be truly successful, companies need to have a corporate mission that is bigger than making a profit. —Marc Benioff, Salesforce

+ We have to bring this world back to sanity and put the greater good ahead of self-interest. —Paul Polman, Unilever

+ Essentially being a for-profit creates opportunity for doing greater good. And financial success as a for-profit with a social conscious carries greater credibility with your peers, potentially influencing actions of other businesses. —Brian Walker, Herman Miller

+ When you're surrounded by people who share a passionate commitment around a common purpose, anything is possible. — Howard Schultz, Starbucks

---

7. "The Upside of a Tradeoff," Jason Fried, Inc., November 1, 2017, https://www.scribd.com/article/361827441/The-Upside-Of-A-Tradeoff.

- Just as people cannot live without eating, so a business cannot live without profits. But most people don't live to eat, and neither must businesses live just to make profits. —John Mackey, Whole Foods

- Money motivates neither the best people, nor the best in people. It can move the body and influence the mind, but it cannot touch the heart or move the spirit; that is reserved for belief, principle, and morality. —Dee Hock, Visa

- People want to do well and do good. They want to understand how they're making a difference in the world. Things change all the time, but your organization's purpose transcends any individual product or service. —Mark Weinberger, EY, formerly Ernst & Young

- The real goal of what we're doing is to have a positive impact on the world. —Ed Catmull, Pixar[8]

THE FUNDAMENTALS

Lest I give the impression that leaders should always have their minds in the clouds of transcendent purposes, let me bring us back to earth. For every agenda item in a staff meeting, people shouldn't get up from the table until three things are settled: who, what, and when. Or to put them together: *Who does what by when?*

FOR EVERY AGENDA ITEM IN A STAFF MEETING, ALWAYS ASK, "WHO DOES WHAT BY WHEN?"

I've seen leaders passionately communicate a new idea and at the end, look at their teams and ask, "Are all of you on board? Do you get it?" They all nod and mumble their assurances, but nothing happens because those three fundamentals haven't been determined. Everyone's responsibility is no one's responsibility.

---

8. These quotes and others are cited at "The Purpose Effect: Inspiring Quotes about a Higher Purpose," May 7, 2016, http://www.danpontefract.com/inspiring-ceo-quotes-about-a-higher-purpose.

When I see this happen, I privately ask the leader, "Can I give you in one sentence everything you would have gotten from an MBA? I guarantee it will make you and your team far more productive." He or she inevitably wants to know and I say, "For each item you want accomplished, ask, 'Who does what by when?' Before you move from one item to the next, ask this question and settle these issues. If you do, your people will have direction and you'll have confidence. If you don't, I can assure you that very little, if anything, will happen."

For some leaders, this is a revolutionary concept! They've never used it before and they've never seen it used. This question can instantly transform their delegation from cloudy to clear and eliminate the vast majority of confusion and frustration—for their team members and for them. Giving a responsibility to a *group* seldom works. Each assignment must be owned by *an individual*, who may certainly enlist the participation of others, but this person is ultimately responsible. "Who" is responsibility, "what" is clarity, and "when" is the deadline.

THE *TOP* OF YOUR GAME

As I consult with leaders, it's often helpful to point them to three distinct areas of their thinking. To be successful, they need to be at least proficient in all three. Most of them excel in one or two of these, but few excel in all of them. I tell them, "This will help you play at the TOP of your game." We look at the *tactical, organizational,* and *personal* areas of their leadership.

TACTICAL

Many leaders are outstanding at thinking, planning, and delegating. They don't mind getting "deep in the weeds" of their organizations. This area deals with:

+ Finances
+ Facilities
+ Leadership development implementation
+ Recruiting and staffing
+ Modes of communication

- ✦ Planning

- ✦ Reporting

Each of these may have begun as abstract concepts in the leader's mind, but they soon take concrete shape with clear direction, assignments, and deadlines. This is the vision in running shoes.

ORGANIZATIONAL

Before the tactical plans develop, leaders conceptualize their direction. This is where the dreams take shape. They know their vision won't just happen, so they devise a vehicle to take them there. The vehicle is the organizational chart, the products and processes, the values, and the culture. In this area of thinking, leadership selection and development strategies are paramount. These will be implemented tactically, but they are conceptualized globally. I tell pastors, "A healthy church is pastor-led, staff-driven, board-empowered, and congregationally-informed." The same big picture concept can be applied to businesses and nonprofit organizations.

PERSONAL

Some leaders are so devoted to their organizational goals that they neglect their own emotional and relational health and they don't devote time and resources for personal development. At the beginning, they may have found a friend or two with a similar vision, and they started their company in a garage or a living room. After a while, growth has exponentially compounded the demands on their time, energy, and talents. To stay sane—or become sane again—leaders need to ask some crucial questions:

- ✦ Who's holding my ladder? Who do I need to have holding my ladder?

- ✦ In what areas am I growing? In what areas am I stagnant or sliding backwards?

- ✦ Where do I need to engage more fully? Where do I need to disengage?

- ✦ What skills need to be sharpened?

- ✦ What stresses need to be noticed and reduced?

- What pains haven't been healed yet?

- How much are finances (or lack of them) putting a strain on me?

- How much of my time and energy are spent trying to solve the same problems again and again?

- What people and activities are the most satisfying?

- What people and activities are the most draining?

- What are necessary and regular sources of fresh ideas and encouragement?

- How much am I really listening when others are talking to me?

- How much am I authentic and how much am I playing a role?

- Who is a friend I can be honest with and count on?

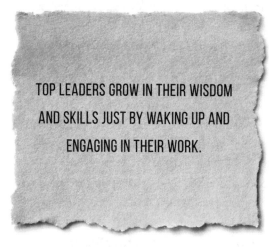

TOP LEADERS GROW IN THEIR WISDOM AND SKILLS JUST BY WAKING UP AND ENGAGING IN THEIR WORK.

All of us have holes in our leadership. After all, we're thoroughly human. Our success is very often limited by our inability (or unwillingness) to be objective about our strengths and the deficits in our tactical, organizational, and personal plans and implementation. Asking hard questions invites us to stop and think. Thinking more clearly is essential for good leadership.

THE WISDOM GAP

In virtually every organization I've encountered over many decades, I've noticed that the gap between the CEO or senior pastor and the next level of leadership is always significant—and often huge. Top leaders grow in their wisdom and skills just by waking up and engaging in their work. They're forced to have high-level conversations, think high-level thoughts, and make high-level decisions. They listen to challenging podcasts and read inspiring books. They meet top leaders in their communities and from around the world. They grow without even trying.

In the next level, leaders are focused on implementing tasks that were assigned at executive staff meetings. They're primarily doers, not thinkers. They're consumed with tactical thoughts, plans, and activities. Their meetings, lunches, and relationships are with people at their level and below them. If they're self-motivated, they listen to podcasts and read books, but their focus is fundamentally different than the top leader. The people at this level are implementers.

Over and over again, top leaders shake their heads and tell me, "I'm tired of doing all the thinking!" These leaders often don't realize that the people who report to them are tired of doing all the doing. As the organization grows, the gap between the top leaders and the second level often gets even wider. It is unrealistic for top leaders to eliminate the gap entirely, but they can narrow it. Let me offer a few suggestions:

+ To make assignments clear so tension is reduced, for every agenda item, the leader needs to ask, "Who does what by when?"

+ When the top leader reads a particularly insightful book, he can recommend the team read it and talk about it together.

+ When the leader reads an article or listens to a podcast that inspires vision or provides practical steps toward progress, he can send links to the team.

+ When the leader signs up for a conference, she can take the team and they can debrief afterward so they're all on the same page.

+ The leader can set aside three meetings a year (just meetings, not retreats) to specifically talk about helping everyone on the team to grow in organizational thinking and therefore narrow the wisdom gap.

+ The leader can set aside one hour every six months with each person on the team to talk about two things: the person's obvious, exemplary skills as well as anything that's limiting him or her from excelling even more.

- The leader can hire a personal coach to spend time with the people on the team to equip them, affirm them, and help them grow.

- Once a year, the leader's personal coach can meet with the team to give them encouragement and point out ways they can work together more effectively.

- To be more approachable and authentic, for fifteen minutes in every staff meeting, the leader can share personal perspectives, hopes, and struggles.

These are very simple but effective means to close the wisdom gap... but only if you use them.

Every time we make a significant purchase for our homes or offices, we receive a user manual. Dishwashers, microwaves, televisions, games, cars, printers, and computers all come with them. A friend gave me a pen that was so complicated, it came with directions!

I've suggested to some leaders that they create a user manual so their teams will know how to relate to them and narrow the gap even more. They've given these to their staffs and said, "This is how you can get the most out of your relationship with me." For a few of my clients, I wrote a "user's manual" that the CEOs used to help their teams. It includes these components:

1. This is how I think...

2. This how I want things done...

3. This is how you can diplomatically give me new ideas...

4. This is how and why I promote people...

5. This is how I measure success...

6. These are the people I pay close attention to...

7. This is what's most important to me...

8. This is how to relate to my family...

9. This how to tell me you want to leave and start your own company or organization...

10. This is how to tell me you want to just leave...

11. If you have a problem with me, this is how to approach me...

12. If you have a problem with your job, this is how to handle it...

13. This is how I respond when you're not responsible...

14. This is how I respond when you make honest mistakes...

15. This is how to respectfully disagree with me...

16. This is how I communicate most effectively...

My friend Rob Ketterling, pastor of River Valley Church in Minneapolis, Minnesota, has expanded this brief outline to prepare his staff for conversations about getting the most out of their relationship with him. He plans to use this "how to" guide for onboarding new hires as well as equipping his staff to relate to him more effectively.[9]

I suggest you carve out at least a couple of hours to go over your own user's guide with your team. You'll need plenty of time to explain your points and they'll want to ask a lot of questions! It will almost certainly be eye-opening for them and it'll probably be just as revelatory for you as you realize how little they've understood you.

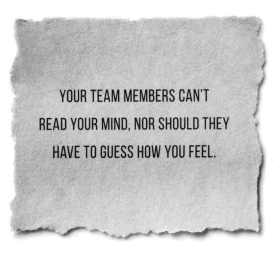

YOUR TEAM MEMBERS CAN'T READ YOUR MIND, NOR SHOULD THEY HAVE TO GUESS HOW YOU FEEL.

Do you think your team members can read your mind? They can't. Do you think they should have to guess how you feel and respond to different situations? They shouldn't. Much of the wisdom gap is born out of ignorance created by the lack of communication. You won't close it—in fact, you don't want to close it completely—but you can narrow the gap so they understand you far better than they do now. Perhaps the best training you can give your team is to teach them to think more effectively—about their roles, about the team, and about you as their leader.

---

9. See Appendix.

THINK ABOUT IT...

1. For your organization, how would you answer these questions:

   > Where is "there"?

   > How will you know when you're there?

   > What are the intermediate benchmarks of progress?

2. What are some strategies to use so you and your team don't lose focus during "the muddy middle" between the beginning and the end of a project?

3. Do you agree or disagree with the statement: "Your gut is smarter than your head?" When has this been true for you? When has trusting reason alone gotten you into trouble?

4. What are some ways you can tell if your organization has congruence? And if it doesn't?

5. How would it help you and your team if every agenda item discussed was followed by your question, "Who does what by when?"

6. Which of the suggestions about closing the wisdom gap will help you lead more effectively? What do you think the results will be for your team and for you?

3

WHOSE ORGANIZATION IS THIS?
THE QUESTION OF OWNERSHIP

Connect the dots between individual roles and the goals of the
organization. When people see that connection,
they get a lot of energy out of work. They feel the importance,
dignity, and meaning in their job.
—Ken Blanchard

My friend Mike Robertson and I were in Johannesburg, South
Africa, for an event. On the day before a formal dinner, Mike realized he
hadn't packed the right pair of shoes for the occasion. He asked me if I'd
like to go shopping with him. I was sure it was going to be much more than
a mere shopping trip, so I was glad to go.

We walked to a mall next to our hotel and we went into a men's clothing store. I saw plenty of shoes that I thought were perfectly acceptable,
but through a process of logical deduction, I soon concluded that Mike
had a very particular type of shoe in mind: black with shades of brown
and two buckles on the side. He was very specific and it appears the shoes
were particularly rare. We went from store to store, but no one had what he
wanted. By this time, the stores were closing, but Mike still was shoeless. I

was amused as I tagged along and watched him examine every shoe in the city...or so it seemed.

As shopkeepers were closing their doors or pulling gates across the front of their stores, Mike finally saw the shoes he'd been looking for in a store display window. The saleswoman had already closed the door to the shop and she was turning the sign from "Open" to "Closed." Mike knocked on the window to get her attention. He spoke loud enough for her to hear, "I know you're closing, but could I look at those shoes?" He pointed to the pair he had his eye on. It was his last shot.

The lady smiled, unlocked the door, opened it, and said, "Come on in."

For a long time, she brought out different sizes of the style for Mike to try on. He wasn't in a hurry and it was obvious the lady wasn't at all upset at having to stay after closing time. The two of them were intently and happily engaged in finding Mike the shoes that were exactly right.

After a long while, as Mike was trying on yet another pair, I said to her, "Let me guess. You own this shop, don't you?"

She looked a little surprised and asked, "How did you know?"

"Oh," I responded. "It's obvious."

If she had been an hourly employee, she would have been looking at the clock as the minutes counted down to closing time. She would have ignored Mike's plea to stay open, or she would have told him, "You'll have to come back tomorrow."

The perspective of an owner is very different from an employee's. An owner thinks, *Whatever it takes, I'll make things work out.* But an employee wants to do the least work with minimal inconvenience—and still get paid. Owners realize others are dependent on them for their livelihood, but employees see themselves as followers, not leaders to take charge for the sake of others.

THINKING LIKE OWNERS

When I meet with business leaders, executives, employees, and volunteers, I'm looking for people who think like owners, not like employees. That may sound confusing since most of the people who work in businesses are employees and those who serve in churches are staff members or volunteers. But I'm defining the term broadly. By my definition, "owners" are *people who have a vested interest in the organization's mission.* They go above and beyond the minimum requirements to get a job done. They care, they devote their time and passion, and they aren't easily satisfied. By this definition, every person can "own" the vision, the mission, and the goals. "Employees" don't think like owners. They show up for their own benefits, complain when things aren't to their liking, and do the minimum (or less) of what's expected of them. Owners put in more than people might expect; employees put in as little as possible.

OUR TASK AS LEADERS IS TO TRANSFORM EMPLOYEES SO THEY THINK LIKE OWNERS, CARE LIKE OWNERS, AND INVEST THEIR TALENTS LIKE OWNERS.

Many employees are focused on narrowly defined, repeatable tasks; they often fail to see how their part fits into the larger mission of the organization. An employee has a limited, specific job to perform, but an owner has a broad responsibility to advance the organization. Our task as leaders, then, is to transform employees into owners. Every person who is part of our business can think like an owner, care like an owner, and invest their talents like an owner.

Let me give a couple of examples.

I've been in many churches where the greeters, ushers, multimedia technicians, teachers, and childcare workers show up faithfully, but they don't connect the dots between what they do and the people who come to church every week. But I know some outstanding pastors who make it their aim to turn all of these people into owners. They create opportunities to explain to the volunteers how their service has a profound impact on people and helps them grow in faith.

I've watched some business leaders who were bright and competent, but for different reasons, they created an elitist mentality. Maybe they feel superior because they've risen out of the ranks or maybe they believe they're inherently better than others. Who knows? They assign specific tasks and tell people on their teams to concentrate on their single cog in the corporate machine. In these companies, creative, passionate people feel restricted and unappreciated, and they long to know their contribution matters. But I've also known some top executives whose philosophy of leadership is to instill vision and passion from the executive suite all the way to the front desk. They spend time imagining what will motivate every person to give his or her best to fulfill the mission of the company and they devote considerable time to cultivate this vision in everyone. They do a great job of turning employees into men and women who have caught the leader's heart and have become owners of the company's goals.

It's not enough to pay people a fair wage for their work and thank them for their service. Great leaders teach their people—all of their people—the value of the vision. Imparting this perspective takes time and skill. One of the most important roles of leadership is to move people beyond merely completing tasks so they are empowered to perform those tasks with greater vision, passion, and creativity.

OBJECTIVES AND KEY RESULTS

Earlier, I mentioned the value of creating specific objectives and key results (OKRs) for people throughout any organization. These documents would take the place of the normal job descriptions most companies use, sometimes called key performance indices (KPIs). By their very nature, OKRs force people to think more deeply and broadly than the list of tasks often associated with job descriptions. There's a big difference between job descriptions and job responsibilities. If we think more expansively, we'll see that some people need detailed job descriptions, but everyone has job responsibilities. The question is: if each person doesn't do his or her job, what will *not* get done?

In a job description, success is achieved by checking completed items off a list, often without reference to the impact of those tasks on higher goals in the organization. OKRs identify responsibilities. They connect the dots between the role each person is assigned with the larger, more motivating mission of the company. Every activity, then, is part of the larger whole and each activity can be seen as crucial to fulfill the organization's purpose. With OKRs, there are fewer employees and far more owners. Leaders continually connect the dots for every person. Those who continue to have a limited perspective can receive additional attention to correct their thinking, or they may need to find another company where the leaders want people to accomplish limited tasks instead of thinking and acting like owners.

Leaders can certainly communicate the objectives for each person's responsibilities: these are the specific tasks to be performed. But they should go farther to enumerate the key results: the impact these roles will have on the organization. An administrative assistant will have a detailed list of tasks and a flow chart of how documents and other information is to be routed, but will become an owner when the leader makes sure the assistant grasps the importance of this work for everyone involved. The *objective* is to move communication effectively; the *key results* are to make the organization more powerful and effective in the lives of customers.

Whose organization is it? Who owns it? In the healthiest organizations, the ones where the leaders are thinking accurately, everyone is an owner, or is in the process of becoming an owner. When this happens, the primary goal of each person every day is no longer just to make money, but to make a difference—doing well while doing good.

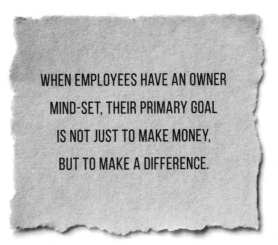

WHEN EMPLOYEES HAVE AN OWNER MIND-SET, THEIR PRIMARY GOAL IS NOT JUST TO MAKE MONEY, BUT TO MAKE A DIFFERENCE.

Many leaders are thrilled if a few of their staff members act like owners, but that's not enough. If everyone else sees themselves as employees who are only completing limited tasks, the leader will end up exerting an enormous amount of effort to produce frustrating results. The leader must create a culture in which all employees realize that what they do has a profound impact on the organization. If they feel what they are doing has value and meaning, it will resonate internally and with their customers.

In a church, even those who are served can become owners when they sense everyone working and praying together for a higher purpose. Newcomers may tell their neighbors, "You won't believe what I experienced last Sunday in church! I can't wait to go back there!" They may not be able to articulate the specifics of an ownership culture, but that's what they sensed when they walked through the door.

When pastors instill a sense of ownership into their people, financial investing becomes a recognizable sign that people have bought into the vision of the church. They give because they believe in the mission. Today, many people move in and out of churches without landing in one because nothing has captured their hearts. They don't give because they don't feel connected.

Almost all leaders have spent considerable time crafting a vision statement, which they see as compelling. From my point of view, a vision is only compelling when people throughout the organization see themselves as an integral part of fulfilling it. If they remain detached observers who participate in only a handful of activities, they'll have a myopic perspective and have little passion. But if they're convinced their contribution of time and skills will help to propel the organization to accomplish its goals, they'll be highly motivated. Far too many leaders spend more time crafting the vision statement than pushing it into the lives of people throughout the organization.

It doesn't happen naturally or easily. Communicating the core values of the organization is a labor of love to intrigue minds and capture hearts. It takes a lot of effort, but it's well worth it. The leader's responsibility isn't only to craft the vision, nor is it only to communicate the vision. The leader's bigger responsibility is to impart it so effectively that the most people have the greatest desire to fulfill it.

A good vision statement is never about the product or service; it focuses on the benefits to the consumer, creating a community and adding value to people's lives. An easy way to tell if people are owners or employees is to ask them, "What would happen to the organization and the people if you didn't fulfill your responsibilities?" If they don't know, have a vague answer, or their response is only about the impact on them, they're employees. But if their eyes widen and they say, "Well, it would have a domino effect. This wouldn't happen and that wouldn't happen and the vision would be set back. We can't let that happen!" This person has the heart and thought processes of an owner.

SNAPSHOT

We get a glimpse of the heart of leaders when we hear them making a pitch to recruit new staff members. If they talk to the prospective new hire like he or she is a family member, the leader is an owner who is already casting a vision for that person to become an owner, too. But if the leader only talks about the tasks to perform and money—both of which are important, but not ultimately important—the leader is thinking like an employee and is recruiting people to only become employees.

Business leaders with an eye on a bigger, better future see potential in others. They can imagine someone serving effectively in this role or that one and they're excited about casting a vision of how the person can have a greater impact. They see beyond their own function; they have the bigger picture, so they're always looking for others who will own a part of the vision.

The best leaders live for a higher purpose than statistics. Numbers matter, but only if they reflect significant impact. These people aren't defensive or possessive; they're glad to share power because they know they need others to accomplish the higher good. And they're glad to share decision-making because they've learned that others have great ideas. I'm not suggesting a muddled decision-making process. When I meet with my team, I tell them, "I'll make the final decision, but I want to hear your ideas first. Bring me your best and we'll see where it leads."

People who think like owners are eager to share credit because they've also shared the risks and responsibilities for the outcome. When something doesn't work out, they don't jockey for position so they can blame someone else. They realize they all participated in the decision and the process, so they can all learn something from the results.

At all levels of a business, leaders who are captured by the purpose of the organization regularly think about succession. They're imagining who would replace them—and do an even better job. Succession isn't just about the exit of one person and the entrance of another; it's about the organization's sustainability. So, a greeter notices when others give them eye contact and a friendly response. A manager looks for people who are eager to learn new skills and get along well with others. Childcare volunteers notice when a parent is especially interested in how the class is run.

In every field and at every level, employees have myopia and see only their task today. But owners have a microscope and a telescope—they see the potential in particular people who catch their eye and they look into the future to recognize needs long before those needs surface. They know that part of their responsibility is to find outstanding people who will expand the work in the present and continue it in the future.

Every leader I've ever known would instantly claim to be an owner, but far fewer of them have the intentional goal of making every person in their company an owner. I'm convinced that much of the lethargy and conflict leaders endure from their people are the direct result of those people acting like employees rather than owners. In organizations that share power, decision-making, and credit, people are more flexible and more creative; they need less control and they get more done; and they attract the best people because they really love what they do every day. These people think and act like owners only because their leader created the environment and tenaciously communicated the organization's values. It's that simple—and it's that important.

> PEOPLE THINK AND ACT LIKE OWNERS ONLY BECAUSE THEIR LEADER CREATED THE ENVIRONMENT AND TENACIOUSLY COMMUNICATED THE ORGANIZATION'S VALUES.

CREATING CONNECTIONS

What turns employees into owners? What can leaders do to motivate their people to share their vision and passion? Some of us are tired of trying to connect with our executive team or staff members, so we go directly to those who are most pliable: our frontline workers or customers. However, we won't motivate the people on our teams by going around them. We'll only turn them into owners if we take time to know them, uncover their desires, and show them how the organization's vision will help to fulfill their dreams.

In an article for *Inc.* magazine, entrepreneur Gary Vaynerchuk explains his secret to motivate people who work for his companies. He insists, "Workers are more important than clients" and explains, "Having taken two businesses from $3 million to $60 million in revenue, each in less than five years, I've learned that employee happiness and well-being come before everything else—including signing on new clients."

Many top executives, Vaynerchuk observes, complain that their people aren't as committed to the company as they are. He believes that's "a ludicrous expectation." But he doesn't give up on his commitment to motivate them to buy into the company as much as possible. He uses a process of "reverse engineering." Instead of telling them what he wants from them, he asks them what they want from the company. He explains, "Everyone has different drivers (or passions), so you have to use your ears and listen: What's her ambition? What does he want to do with his life?" As he had these conversations, he discovered powerful desires he wouldn't have uncovered if he had only sent out emails updating the vision statement and encouraging people to work harder.

As his companies grew, Vaynerchuk soon realized he couldn't meet with hundreds of people, but he made sure his top executives followed his model of building and deepening relationships. In this way, every team member and every new hire gets personal attention and each one has the opportunity to talk with an executive to connect their hopes and dreams to the organization's vision.

Vaynerchuk concludes:

> I refer to myself as an HR-driven CEO. I thrive under the pressure of having the entire business on my shoulders, and I feel a responsibility to keep my workers happy, not as a group, but as individuals. I develop my relationships with my employees and put in the time to learn what is most wanted from me as their CEO, because that will result in their caring about my company. It's about building trust, and trust has to be earned. Put in the effort to make your people happy, and you will grow faster.[10]

---

10. "Employees Are More Important Than Clients," an interview with Gary Vaynerchuk, *Inc.*, May 31, 2016, https://www.inc.com/magazine/201606/gary-vaynerchuk/prioritizing-employee-happiness.html.

Workers represent the culture and the brand of the organization: they are the most effective advertisement for its health and vision. The brand isn't the logo or the website; it's the attitude of the people who are integrally connected to the organization. The source of growth isn't the customers. Businesses grow because the people who are committed to the values and vision pull out all the stops to reach out to new people. The attitudes and actions of workers, staff members, and volunteers either attract or repel—they seldom have a neutral impact.

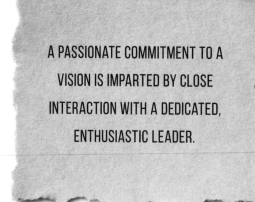

A PASSIONATE COMMITMENT TO A VISION IS IMPARTED BY CLOSE INTERACTION WITH A DEDICATED, ENTHUSIASTIC LEADER.

Workers don't buy into a leader's vision because they get regular updates or sit in on meetings. A passionate commitment to a vision is imparted by close interaction with a dedicated, enthusiastic leader. Your people will never be as dedicated and single-minded as you are, but if they understand that you genuinely care about them and their dreams, they'll realize their dreams are consistent with yours—and they'll become owners. Invest time in getting to know them. Find out what makes them excited and creative. Connect their passion to your vision.

THINK ABOUT IT...

1. Describe the difference in how this chapter defines "owners" and "employees."

2. What are some benefits of connecting objectives (the nuts and bolts of a job) with key results (the multiplied impact of that work), instead of giving people a job description of tasks to perform?

3. Have you served in an organization where most of the people thought and acted like employees? How did this affect relationships and productivity?

4. Have you served where the leader created a compelling vision and cast it attractively so people eagerly told others about it? How did this affect relationships and productivity?

5. Write a plan to connect with your staff members' dreams so you can transform them from employees to owners.

6. What steps of progress will you look for?

4

WHO AM I?
THE QUESTION OF IDENTITY

What you think means more than anything else in your life—
more than what you earn, more than where you live,
more than your social position, and more than what anyone
else may think about you.
—George Matthew Adams

I meet with some of the most successful leaders in the United States
and around the world. They have incredible talents and have seen remarkable growth in their organizations. But when I peel back some layers of
their obvious competencies, I often notice a striking similarity: many of
them live with a significant measure of insecurity. It shows up in comparison, competition, and flashes of self-doubt. I've learned to recognize this
often-buried but common trait in leaders because I've struggled with it
myself.

It seems we are seldom satisfied. People with dark skin (like me) wish
we had lighter skin, but those with light skin sometimes spend a lot of
money and time to get a tan. People with straight hair want curly hair and
those who have curls want straight hair—but most who are bald would

take any kind of hair! I have a friend who wears a toupee. I'm afraid it's a little too obvious, but he doesn't care. He laughs, saying, "What God has not wrought, I have bought."

THE SEARCH FOR SECURITY

All of us instinctively ask the penetrating question, "Who am I?" Few people, however, come to satisfying answers. We all have inestimable value, but we continue to look for security in something else—anything else!

- We long to be seen as successful and we're haunted by the prospect of failure.

- We live for affirmation and we wilt when we're ignored or criticized.

- We admire people who have great wealth and we feel deflated— even exposed as a failure—because we don't have as much.

- We think the next step up the ladder will finally give us the fulfillment we long for...and it does, for a few days, and then we feel empty and driven again.

- We compare the size of our organizations to our peers'. We feel superior to some and inferior to others, but pride and shame are poor sources of identity.

All of these longings promise to fill the hole in our hearts and finally put the stamp of validity on our lives. They promise the moon, but they leave us with hands full of dust. Ironically, the experience of success, fame, wealth, and organizational growth doesn't necessarily change a person's self-perception. I know people who have achieved all of these things and still feel they need to prove themselves by building the biggest house, driving the fanciest car, wearing the finest clothes, and going on the most lavish vacations. They're trying to mask their insecurities and they're desperately trying to impress people, so they're always marketing themselves.

Please don't misunderstand me. There's nothing in the world wrong with success, pleasure, approval, or power, as long as those don't define us. When they are products of a life lived out of a full heart of gratitude and the security of God's limitless love, we can thoroughly enjoy them and share our abundance with others.

When we meet people, we usually ask, "What do you do?" A few of us may be genuinely interested in the other person, but most of us, if we're painfully honest, are gauging our self-worth (and maybe our net worth) against the person in front of us. As soon as people tell us their role or profession, we instinctively shift into the mode of analysis: how much money does he make? How does that compare with my income? What can I afford that she can't? What's his next step that I can't take? You would think that people of faith would be immune to this kind of comparison, which is a sure sign of insecurity, but we're not. I heard a lady in church say that she always sits in the front row because she doesn't want to spend the whole service comparing her hair and clothes to people in front of her. The sting of insecurity knows no holidays, seasons, or limitations.

Years ago, I served as the pastor of a small church in Hartford, Michigan, far out in the sticks. We had to travel more than three miles to find the closest blinking street light and the nearest McDonald's was eighteen miles away. I was the only dark-skinned person in the county, so I assume some of the people who attended our church came for the novelty factor.

THE EXPERIENCE OF SUCCESS, FAME, WEALTH, AND ORGANIZATIONAL GROWTH DOESN'T NECESSARILY CHANGE A PERSON'S SELF-PERCEPTION.

One week, a traveling evangelist spoke at a series of meetings at our church. It was a shattering experience for me. He said the same things I'd said to our people dozens of times before, but they acted like it was Pentecost all over again, shouting praise to God and singing hallelujahs.

At first, I was amused, but as the service went on, I got angry. Why were they so moved by this guy but sat on their hands when I spoke every week? Then, I realized the answer: the evangelist walked as he talked and I always stayed behind the pulpit. That was it. That was the secret of his success.

The evangelist left town on Wednesday. The next day, I drove to the nearest Radio Shack. I was on a mission. I walked up to the counter and said, "I need an audio cord—the longest one you have in stock."

The man looked in his catalogue for a minute or two and then he looked up and told me, "We don't have it in stock, but will sixty feet work for you? We can have it in two days."

"Perfect!" I was thrilled.

On Saturday morning, I made the trek back to pick up the cord. It probably weighed twenty pounds, but I didn't care. This was going to be my ticket to stardom! That afternoon, I went to the church and plugged the cord into our sound system. I practiced walking back and forth across the platform, in front of the seats, and down the aisles. To be thoroughly prepared, I wrote instructions in red in my sermon notes: "Move away from the pulpit." "Pick up the microphone." "Start walking." "Go in front of the podium." "Walk down the left aisle." I was sure the power of my message would get through now!

The next morning, I was eager for the singing to be finished. I had business to take care of and I was ready. I followed my notes, walking all over the church as I preached, and was masterful at slinging the cord just right so I could make the turns. I was so happy! Near the end, I had enough presence of mind to shift my focus from my performance to the faces of the congregation. They weren't standing, shouting, or singing. They were looking at me like I'd lost my mind, or maybe an alien had taken residence in their pastor's body! Their body language was teaching me a very important lesson: don't try to be something or someone you're not. Stop comparing. Use and hone your talents. Be yourself. Be your best self, but be yourself.

The promises of success and acclaim are incredibly enticing. Certainly, our culture reinforces the attractions. Every commercial and ad is designed to accomplish two objectives: make us dissatisfied with what we have and make the product or service compellingly appealing. We may not need it, but we have to have it! Our lives are inundated with messages that tell us we simply must have this or that, and always more, not less. Education necessarily assigns grades and class rank to young people. When kids pick teams at recess, someone (that would be me) is the last one chosen. Teenagers are constantly evaluating each other's looks, intelligence, wit, or popularity. As adults, we naturally compare our bank accounts and lifestyles to the scenes in the ads and the people around us. I vividly recall riding in the car with Brenda not long after we were married when we passed a moderately-priced restaurant. Both of us looked longingly at the people walking in and I told her, "That's where affluent people eat." Comparison feels strong, powerful, and even euphoric when we're winning the game, but we play by house rules and we always lose in the end.

Measuring ourselves by how we stack up to others is natural, but it's eventually destructive. In geology, the underlying fact of tectonic insecurity may be hidden for years, but at some point when it's least expected, the damage can be overwhelming. The fault line in the Indian Ocean had existed for many years, but on December 26, 2004, the plates violently shifted. The 9.2-magnitude earthquake under the sea created a 100-foot tsunami that raced in every direction, drowning about a quarter of a million people in fourteen countries.

In the same way, fault lines of insecurity in our lives may be hidden for a long time, but a sudden shock of disappointment or the gradual wear of unrelieved stress can cause a psychological quake that devastates us and those around us. We can be masters at disguising the fault lines. We smile when we're dying inside; we compliment others, hoping they'll return the favor; we drive ourselves to

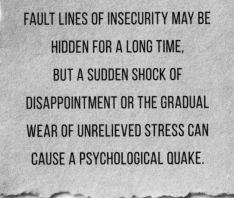

FAULT LINES OF INSECURITY MAY BE HIDDEN FOR A LONG TIME, BUT A SUDDEN SHOCK OF DISAPPOINTMENT OR THE GRADUAL WEAR OF UNRELIEVED STRESS CAN CAUSE A PSYCHOLOGICAL QUAKE.

work long hours to prove we're worthy; we hide from risks or take foolish ones; we deny our fears; we minimize our doubts; and we hope no one has enough insight to look beneath the surface to see what's really going on inside. Sooner or later, however, we can't resist the underlying pressure any longer and the quake strikes. We try to minimize and deflect, but our tidal wave of hurt, fear, shame, and anger washes over the people near us.

SIZE OR IMPACT

Comparisons can consume our thoughts and rob us of joy. Too often, we use the wrong measuring stick. I sometimes talk to leaders who are ashamed of the size of their organizations. They say something like, "I have a small company," or "I'm the pastor of a little church of eighty people." Their tone of voice and the look in their eye tells me they feel embarrassed that they aren't more successful. In their own eyes, they're not measuring up. The question of significance isn't size; it's impact.

Many years ago when I was a pastor, I had a good friend, Edgar Kent, whose church had about twenty-five in attendance on most Sundays. My church had about a hundred and thirty each week, so he thought I had hit the big time. One morning as we had breakfast together, he poured out his confusion and consternation.

"Sam, our church is small. Sometimes, it grows to forty or even fifty, but after a few months, it declines back to twenty-five again. This has happened a dozen times while I've been the pastor. I don't know what's going on."

I picked up a napkin and took a pen out of my pocket. "Edgar, when these people leave your church, where do they go? Do they leave the faith? Do they go to other churches?"

He thought for a few seconds to mentally scan the faces he'd seen in the past few years. "No, they don't leave the faith," he told me. "Some of them are going to other churches and some have started new churches."

Something clicked. I asked, "Tell me who has started churches. What are their names?"

He began naming people who had planted churches. He paused for a few seconds between some of them and then he remembered another...and another. I wrote the names on the napkin. By the time he couldn't remember any others, I had a list of eighteen people who had started churches. I pushed the napkin in front of him and said, "Edgar, God has used you to plant all these churches."

His eyes widened with astonishment. He had never thought of these people in this way. He had seen them as dissatisfied with him and his leadership, not that he had inspired people to establish outposts of God's kingdom in new areas. The size of his church hadn't expanded, but his impact was exponential. Edgar was surprised when I gave him my interpretation of his church's history and actually, he was very reluctant to see the picture I was painting for him. For him, it was literally too good to be true.

Sometimes, we can position ourselves to leverage small size and limited resources for a far greater impact. Brenda's uncle owned a small convenience store far outside any city limits. It was nothing like the huge grocery stores in virtually every city and town today. He had only a few items on his shelves. Near the store was a large immigrant community. These people often had to walk four or five miles to work, but her uncle's store was nearby. People often came into his store, even though the prices were higher than the big stores in town. He was positioned to make an impact on the immigrant community and, in turn, they made an impact on his bottom line.

Some of the most successful companies today have very limited resources: Facebook has more than two billion regular users, but they have no content. Amazon leads the world in sales, but they have no factories or farms. Uber and Lyft are present in cities throughout the world, but they don't own any cars. Airbnb offers accommodations, but they own no property.

These companies have enormous impact, even though they started with only an idea, a vision, and enthusiastic determination. If these leaders had looked at their situations from a normal business perspective, they would never have gotten off the ground. But the thinking of these entrepreneurs wasn't limited by their available resources. They imagined something much greater.

A DIFFERENT QUESTION

We need new metrics to determine our identity. When we answer the identity question with measures of performance, popularity, power, or wealth, we'll remain empty, confused, and desperate—but, of course, we'll try our best to look confident so no one guesses we feel insecure. But there's a far better answer.

We are relational beings. We don't thrive in isolation; in fact, we can't live very long in isolation without going insane. Perhaps a better question than "*Who* am I?" is "*Whose* am I?" Who do I belong to? Who imparts love and meaning to me? Who believes in me no matter what? Who forgives me when I fail and celebrates with me when I succeed?

GOD GAVE THE TORTOISE AND THE HORSE THE SAME AMOUNT OF TIME TO GET INTO NOAH'S ARK.

If we are convinced that God's opinion means more than anyone else's, including our own, we can get off the treadmill of always trying to measure up. We can stop comparing and replace our desperation with gratitude. We may be walking and others may be running, but God gave the tortoise and the horse the same amount of time to get into Noah's Ark. Our journey may have unexpected twists and turns, but God took Joseph on an extended tour of Egypt. (See Genesis 37– 50.) Time and again, those who looked at Joseph failed to see what God saw. His brothers saw him as a useless dreamer. The Midianite traders saw him as a source of profit. Potiphar saw him as a gifted slave. Potiphar's wife saw a potential lover. The prison warden saw him as a hopeless case. But all of them were wrong. God saw Joseph as the future prime minister whose spiritual maturity and organizational skill would save two nations: the Egyptians and his family, which would become the nation of Israel. God's perspective of Joseph was far more accurate and far more import-ant than the view of any person. God often sees things that we don't see. Throughout the Bible, where others saw limitations, God saw potential:

+ God doesn't care about age so He blessed Abraham and Sarah. (See Genesis 21:2.)

+ God doesn't care about fluency. He picked ineloquent Moses to lead His people out of Egypt. (See Exodus 4:10.)

+ God doesn't care about experience. He selected David, a shepherd boy, to become king. (See 1 Samuel 16:1, 12.)

+ God doesn't care about gender. He chose Esther to be queen and save her people. (See Esther 2:17.)

+ God doesn't care about ethnicity. He put foreigners, Rahab and Ruth, in Jesus's family tree. (See Matthew 1:5.)

+ God doesn't care about a person's past. He picked Paul, who had persecuted Christians, to be His spokesman. (See Acts 9:3–9.)

+ God doesn't care about height. Jesus dined with Zacchaeus, who was short in stature but long in desire to meet Jesus. (See Luke 19:1–6.)

+ God doesn't care about a questionable past. After the resurrection, Jesus first appeared to Mary Magdalene, who once harbored seven demons. (See Luke 8:2.)

+ God doesn't care how badly you've failed. Peter denied he knew Jesus, but he was chosen to lead the early church. (See Matthew 16:18.)

God knows we're slow to get it. We're driven, but in the wrong direction. We're confused, so we make poor decisions. No matter how many times God has told us about His love, His grace, and His purpose for us, we fail to fully grasp it. But He never quits.

Most of us see ourselves in a kind of courtroom every day—the courtroom of public opinion—and our performance is our only evidence. The prosecutors are the people who find fault with what we think, say, and do. To be honest, sometimes we're on that side of the room, blasting ourselves with blame for being so insensitive, ugly, or shallow. We try to plead in our own defense, but it just doesn't work. Then Jesus steps up and says, "Your honor, the price has already been paid. The verdict is already in. My client is completely forgiven."

Do we live like the verdict is still out and we have to plead our case by showing we're acceptable to the people around us? Do we live with nagging guilt and the sense that we're never quite enough? Or are we convinced the verdict is in, the debt is paid, and we've been set free?

The real Judge steps down to adopt us as His own. He tells us, "You are My beloved child in whom I am well pleased." He's not "well pleased" because we've done everything right. He's pleased that we belong to Him!

Instead of performing to earn a good verdict (and defending ourselves when we or others question our performance), we realize someone has taken our place, paid the price we couldn't pay, and has given us a status we could never earn. This is the impact of God's grace in our lives and it changes us from the inside out. We still perform, but for a very different reason. We work, we strive, and we pursue excellence—not to prove ourselves, but out of a deep sense of gratitude and a desire to represent the one who has done so much for us. In these two motivations, there's a world of difference. God's grace, then, is the true source of our security.

When we're secure, we walk out of the courtroom of public opinion and we get off the treadmill of performance to prove ourselves. We no longer have anything to prove, so we can relax. We're no longer competing with other leaders, so we're not threatened when someone is better at something than we are. We used to avoid high-level leaders, but now we seek them out so we can learn from them.

SECURE LEADERS STIMULATE CREATIVITY AND VALUE OTHERS' CONTRIBUTIONS, SO THEY ATTRACT THE BEST AND BRIGHTEST.

Insecure leaders don't attract the very best employees and staff. Secure, sharp people don't want to work for insecure leaders. These leaders won't give credit to others, don't affirm creativity and boldness, and are threatened when others receive praise. Insecure leaders cut others off in meetings, claim others' ideas as their own, and patronize people, treating them like children.

Secure leaders are just the opposite. They stimulate creativity and value others' contributions, so they attract the best and brightest. These leaders aren't afraid to look in the mirror and be honest about what they see and they look out the window at the horizons to lead their organizations into the future. They aren't consumed with inflating or guarding their reputations, so they can focus on the people around them to teach, affirm, encourage, and direct.

Leaders who have inner composure realize they stand tall on the shoulders of those who have come before them. They live with a wonderful blend of courage and humility, passion and compassion. They aren't crushed by criticism and they don't resist people who speak the truth to them. They have cultivated the fine art of listening; they understand that to go higher, farther, and faster, they need the input of other secure leaders. They aren't obsessed with controlling people and programs. They hire carefully, delegate clearly, and then let others fly.

BUT WHAT ABOUT...?

Do we understand the concept of God's grace and believe it applies to us at the deepest level of our hearts? Grace is an exceptionally hard concept to grasp. Martin Luther spent his life trying to communicate grace to everyone who would read his books and listen to his messages. He said grace is at the heart of our faith in God. "Faith is a living, daring confidence in God's grace, so sure and certain that a man could stake his life on it a thousand times," he said. But he also recognized our natural desire to prove ourselves instead of trusting in God's grace. He told church leaders that it is necessary for them to study grace, know it well, "teach it unto others, and beat it into their heads continually."[11]

We aren't consciously resistant to God's grace, but many of us think it's too good to be true, or painful experiences in our past scream that God can't love us unconditionally, or we'd rather earn approval from God and others instead of receiving it as a gift. Before we go any farther, we need to address this issue. For some, this is the most important point in this book. We want to experience God's grace, we want to be secure, and we want to lead others with grace instead of guilt and fear. Somehow, our nagging doubts cast a dark shadow over the wonder of God's limitless love and acceptance.

God's magnificent grace isn't something He dispenses once when we become believers and then we're on our own. Pastor Rick Warren observed, "What gives me the most hope every day is God's grace; knowing that His grace is going to give me the strength for whatever I face, knowing that nothing is a surprise to God." If God's grace is so amazing, why is it so

11. Martin Luther, *St. Paul's Epistle to the Galatians* (Philadelphia: Smith, English & Co., 1860), 206.

elusive? We need to boldly ask ourselves, *What prevents me from letting the grace of God penetrate the deepest crevices of my soul?* This isn't a book on psychology, but it doesn't have to be. We simply need to be honest about our penchant to earn approval and open our hearts to God's love.

THE REMEDY

The principles of identity apply to the people you're leading, but first, they apply to you. Let me give you a process to identify and replace "stinkin' thinkin'" with the truth about who you are and whose you are. You can choose the content of your thoughts and your self-concept.

FIRST, NOTICE YOUR COMPULSIONS AND FEARS

As you've read this chapter, have you identified with the paragraphs about comparison and competition, with the ones about fear-driven compulsions to please people or dominate them, with those about defensiveness and control? Sure, you have. Admit it. Don't rush past these observations. Live with them. Ask follow up questions like, "Where did that perspective come from?" and "How has it affected my relationships?" Quite often, leaders are so focused on the future that they don't pay attention to the voices from the past. We don't want to live in the past, but the past can haunt us if we don't address the pains and sins that are buried there. Let them surface. Yes, it's uncomfortable, but it's good for you. Take plenty of time. There's no hurry. And be sure to tell a trusted friend.

FLUSH THE WASTE

Too often, we've let toxic thoughts linger far too long. They haven't just sat there. They've poisoned our relationships and been a constant stink we've learned to live with. Don't live with them any longer. Get rid of them by forgiving those who hurt you, experiencing forgiveness for your wrongs, grieving the losses, and healing the hurts. Again, this takes time, but it consists of dozens of intentional decisions to get rid of the waste in your mind.

CONTINUALLY FILL UP

Find books, podcasts, articles, and messages on the amazing, unconditional love of God. Let people who have struggled to believe it tell you how they finally experienced the wonder of God's grace. You aren't alone. It's hard for all of us to grasp, but it's necessary to dedicate ourselves to pursue it.

GUARD YOUR MIND AND HEART

The second law of thermodynamics tells us that everything in nature, including our grasp of spiritual truth, tends toward randomness and decay. If we don't pay attention, our grasp of God's grace as the source of our security will atrophy, too. (That's what has happened to some of us. We experienced God's love and presence in powerful ways years ago, but the stresses of leadership and unfinished business from the past have slowly eroded our sense that the verdict is in and we're God's beloved children.) We need to be on guard to prevent slipping back into the inevitable insecurity of living for approval, power, and success.

IDENTITY AND SECURITY

When I speak on the topic of identity and security, I often ask someone in the audience to hand me a $20 bill. I ask the audience, "Who would like me to give this to you?" Everyone is eager to get the money. I then put it in my hand and crumple it into a wad. I turn to the crowd and ask, "If I take this to the bank, would they give me $18 for it?" They shake their heads, so I ask if they still want the bill and the response is the same. I then drop the bill on the floor and stomp on it. When I pick it up, it's unrecognizable as a form of money. I tell them, "Maybe the bank would only give me $10 for it now." They laugh because they know that's not true. I ask the audience the question again and they all still want the money.

I tell them, "My friends, you have witnessed and now understand a valuable lesson. No matter what I did to the $20 bill, it didn't decrease in value and you still wanted it. Many times in our lives, we're crumpled, dropped, and ground into the dirt by the decisions we've made, the decisions others have made, the opinions of others, or circumstances beyond our control. We may feel worthless, but our value to God hasn't changed at all. We are created in His image, and we are still called to bear His image to a lost and broken world. You are special. Don't forget that! Never let yesterday's disappointments overshadow today's grace or tomorrow's dreams."

THINK ABOUT IT...

1. What are a dozen ways people try to win approval from those around them? (You can probably list many more than that!)

2. Describe the impact of advertising on our expectations that the next product or service will satisfy us. What do these ads promise? What is the impact of these promises on our desires and expectations?

3. How is the question, "*Whose* am I?" different from "*Who* am I?" Why does this distinction matter in your life?

4. What are some reasons grace is so difficult to grasp, for most people if not for you?

5. What are various characteristics of insecure leaders? What internal messages do they hear that create this insecurity?

6. What are characteristics of secure leaders? What messages do they hear in their minds and hearts?

7. What do you need to do to apply "the remedy"? Be specific.

5

WHAT IS MY ADDRESS?
THE QUESTION OF GEOGRAPHY

There are two primary choices in life: to accept conditions as they
exist or accept the responsibility for changing them.
—Denis Waitley

Quite often, when I talk to business leaders, they say something like,
"We've grown a little where we are, but if we could move our operations to
Dallas"—or Los Angeles, Nashville, Atlanta, or some other bustling city
in the U.S. or a major metropolis in another country—"I'm sure we'd be
much bigger." These leaders have heard talks from leaders in those cities,
they've read articles about explosive growth, and they're convinced they
need to move there. They live with the nagging question of geography:
where can I thrive?

My advice isn't to just suck it up and stop complaining. Quite the opposite. I tell them to carefully consider their doubts about their current location and their hopes for success somewhere else. The process of thinking
deeply about this issue enables them to take a good, hard look at their
presuppositions. Objectivity helps them to think and plan more clearly
and it lets them consider the implications of a decision without the fog of
confusion.

The question of geography isn't only about the company's current address; it's also about our willingness to embrace specific opportunities beyond that address. For instance, I've been asked to speak at thousands of events. For each one, I'm nervous: I don't know if I have what it takes to connect with the audience. I'm always nervous...and I want to always be nervous. My nervousness and doubts keep me both on my knees and on my toes. They are the best deterrents to arrogance. My psychological disruption causes me to think more specifically about each speaking opportunity, never take any audience for granted, and value each moment in front of them. Emotionally, it would be easier to avoid the geography of the platform, but I'm determined to let my fears sharpen me instead of limiting me.

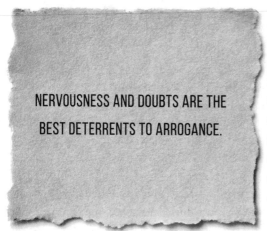

NERVOUSNESS AND DOUBTS ARE THE BEST DETERRENTS TO ARROGANCE.

Sometimes, the geography is overwhelming. I've been asked to speak at some very big events and on those occasions, I've been in green rooms with some of the most gifted and famous leaders in the world. Each time, I instinctively ask myself, *What in the world am I doing here?* And I always have the same answer: *I don't belong here!*

For several decades, psychologists and coaches have identified "the imposter syndrome" as "phoniness in people who believe they are not intelligent, capable, or creative despite evidence of high achievement." In other words, they feel like frauds and they're terrified of being found out. No matter how high they climb, they feel inadequate. Success doesn't resolve the problem. In fact, it makes it worse because more than ever, the person feels like he doesn't belong. In an article for *Forbes*, professional coach Ashley Stahl recommends those who have this problem with their personal geography to "change your mental programming." She writes:

> Reframe your thoughts and realize that what you're feeling isn't founded on anything real. Feelings of inadequacy and fear are all in your head, so imagine how you'd feel if you could turn these

thoughts into something positive. Instead of thinking something like "I don't know *anything*" why not try reframing it to "I don't know *everything*…yet. I'm still learning"? See how it feels when you don't put the pressure on yourself to know it all. After all, no one is perfect.[12]

SWAP ANTS FOR PETS

We may not be able to completely screen out thoughts that create anxiety, but when we recognize them, we can replace them. We can swap ANTS for PETS.[13] ANTS are Automatic Negative Thoughts. They seem to spontaneously appear in our minds, but in reality, they are often the product of years of negative thinking, false assumptions, and enough self-fulfilling prophesies of doom to make us believe they're entirely true. PETs are Performance-Enhancing Thoughts. They renew our hope, stimulate our creativity to find new solutions, and rev our engines to propel us to productive action.

We've had ANTS in our minds for so long that they feel right at home. However, when we doubt that we belong, we can become paralyzed or frenetic, immobilized or stuck in hypersonic speed. We devalue ourselves and we become skeptical of others' motives. When we recognize this kind of self-doubt, we need to take a break for a while to reflect on who we are and what we bring to the table. We need to identify and reject the ANTS and recharge our minds with PETS. For instance:

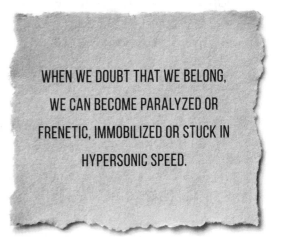

WHEN WE DOUBT THAT WE BELONG, WE CAN BECOME PARALYZED OR FRENETIC, IMMOBILIZED OR STUCK IN HYPERSONIC SPEED.

---

12. "Feel Like A Fraud? Here's How To Overcome It," Ashley Stahl, *Forbes Leadership*, December 10, 2017, https://www.forbes.com/sites/ashleystahl/2017/12/10/feel-like-a-fraud-heres-how-to-overcome-imposter-syndrome/#24ad0f524d31.
13. Adapted from Anthony Grant and Jane Greene, *It's Your Life. What are you going to do with it?* (Great Britain: Pearson Education Limited, 2004), 128.

- Reflect on the past few years and identify your talents, your interests, your passions, and when you felt particularly effective in having an impact on people.

- Think about the same time frame, but this time, identify what has bored you, frustrated you, and drained your energy.

- Consider your present situation. How can you shape it, find mentors and resources, and make it the very best it can be? Or, after careful analysis and wise input, do you conclude you really don't fit there any longer?

Leadership succession is one of those periods when many of us feel out of place. We're planning to change our geography, but we're filled with questions and concerns. I met with a leader who is fifty-two years old and is already looking ten years down the road, when he plans to retire and be replaced. After long discussions, this is one of the points I wrote for him in a follow-up report: "In the next few years, I'd love for you to remain extra self-aware about areas where you find yourself increasingly bored, disengaged, and wishing you didn't have to deal with the issues and people who make you feel that way."

I've seen it happen too many times. Leaders who have given everything in them to the success of an organization gradually feel increasingly out of place in the company or organization they've loved for many years. They no longer feel they belong and they begin to bail out emotionally and mentally before it's time to go. It's like they've sent a change of address form to the post office before they've actually moved.

FOUR CALLINGS

All leaders have four distinct callings. These overlap and intertwine, but it's helpful to understand each one independently.

1. PURPOSE

Based on talents, experiences, and opportunities, leaders live to accomplish something significant. This is what keeps them up at night and gets them up early in the morning. Their work isn't just a job. They don't just put in hours for a paycheck. They know they can have an impact and make a difference in the lives of people. This is what they live for.

2. PASSION

Generally, purpose is a constant, a fixed point in a leader's life, especially by the time they have had enough experiences to sharpen their purpose. But passion is more complex. It's more than education, talent, or experiences. It's the engine that drives the leader to fulfill the purpose.

Some leaders are energized about their own success, their own income, and their own fame. That's certainly a type of passion, but there's a better, higher way. Great leaders have a passion to change lives—even through indirect channels like technology, retail, restaurants, or shipping. They think about the difference their work makes in the daily lives of men and women, young and old, so enthusiasm and energy flow out of them. People love to follow leaders like this.

3. PEOPLE

Leaders invest their hearts and their talents in people at every level of the organization: their executive team, mid-level managers, frontline employees, volunteers, customers, clients, and those who are touched by all those groups. The job, then, isn't about cranking out products or services; it's about touching people and making their lives better.

4. PLACE

A leader will probably have the same purpose and passion wherever he goes, but he must focus on a particular location to invest his heart and hands in having an impact. Leaders need to be convinced *this* is the place, *this* is the time, and *these* are the people where they devote their passions to accomplish their purpose. Clarity about place, then, is essential for the leader to flourish.

We live in a different world than our parents and grandparents knew. The invention of the automobile and the convenience of travel have shown us cities, regions, and nations our ancestors had only seen in books before. Today, mobility is the norm, not the exception. For decades, people looked for greener pastures in the suburbs and millions of people left the inner cities. But the trend is reversing, especially among Millennials. In *TIME*, Sam Frizell notes,

Americans are experiencing an urban renaissance of unanticipated proportions, as young people graduate college and flock to cities, delaying buying a home and perhaps rejecting the suburban ideal altogether. In 2005, multifamily housing accounted for just 17% of all housing starts. In 2013, multifamily housing accounted for fully 33% of starts. Data released last week on housing starts in March reinforce that trend, with multifamily homes, a good portion of it high-rise apartment buildings, accounting for 40% of all new construction.[14]

What do these seemingly arcane statistics mean to leaders? It means mobility is now the norm and we're not immune to the itch to move. That itch is even more intense as we watch our audience and customers make their exodus to bigger cities with more energy and opportunities. Our subconscious conclusion might be: if they're moving, maybe I should, too!

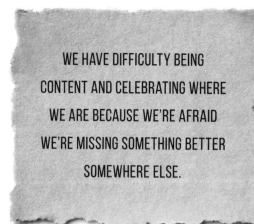

WE HAVE DIFFICULTY BEING CONTENT AND CELEBRATING WHERE WE ARE BECAUSE WE'RE AFRAID WE'RE MISSING SOMETHING BETTER SOMEWHERE ELSE.

In every aspect of our lives, we hear messages that foster discontent with our current situations. We simply must have the next model of phone, the latest year's car, higher speed Internet service, better blooming roses, and the newest fashion in clothes. It's no wonder that the same built-in dissatisfaction often plagues our sense of place. *Next* promises to have more value than *now*. We have difficulty being content and celebrating where we are because we're afraid we're missing something better (maybe much better) somewhere else. We're not satisfied with incremental growth where we are because we dream of quantum leaps somewhere else.

14. "The New American Dream Is Living in a City, Not Owning a House in the Suburbs," Sam Frizell, *TIME*, April 25, 2014, http://time.com/72281/american-housing.

MAYBE IT'S TIME TO GO

All of this isn't to say that we should never consider a move. Where would we be if the explorers hadn't found routes to the New World and around the globe? Where would each country be if men and women hadn't had the courage to settle new lands? Where would our businesses be if intrepid leaders hadn't launched new ideas?

Sometimes, it's time to go.

We may realize we really don't fit where we've been leading and serving. I read an interesting article about bomb-sniffing dogs. The writer noted that bloodhounds have the best sense of smell in the canine world, but we rarely see them sniffing for explosives in airports or on the battlefield. The reason is that this breed is the very best for manhunts, but they get bored too quickly if there's not enough action. Without the excitement of a chase, they become distracted and ineffective.[15] The same characteristics can be true of leaders: We may be tremendously skilled at some area of leadership, but if we're not in the right place, we become like bloodhounds who are in the wrong job. It's time to sniff somewhere else.

Don't make the automatic assumption that if you aren't happy, it must mean it's time to find another address. But at least ask the questions of geography to determine where you belong. There is no merit in being miserable for no good reason. This isn't a rehearsal for life; it's the real thing! Life is too short to waste it in boredom. Every day is a second chance for all of us. What will we do with it?

If leaders are bold and wise enough to ask the questions, many will conclude they're in the right place after all, some will realize they have very limited options for a number of reasons, and more than a few will see enough evidence for a move to warrant the upheaval it inevitably involves.

Some of us live with limitations that life has thrust upon us, so we may not have options to change geography. Brenda and I talked about a couple with a Downs syndrome child. Every day, the parents pour out their love for this baby, but their love is coupled with the realization that they'll need to provide an extraordinary level of care for many years. Whatever the situation—physical illness, emotional disorders, aging parents, addictions, or

---

15. "Ask Marilyn," Marilyn vos Savant, May 15, 2016.

whatever it might be—it brings out a full range of emotions. Sometimes you want to draw that person close to comfort and love, sometimes you're angry and insist life isn't fair, and sometimes you're utterly exhausted with the conflicting feelings and physical demands of caring. In these circumstances, the financial strain is added to the emotional weight and it can be overwhelming.

Most people don't have the financial bandwidth to consider the full range of options about where they will live and what job they might take. People with limited incomes in a part of the country with a moderate cost of living may be barely able to make ends meet. They probably can't move to Newport Beach, California, and buy a house on the beach. Debt is a major problem for many people. A move needs to be a step out of debt, not into it. But even there, creative, determined people can find a way. They may save for six months or a year to afford to live while they look for a job. They may find a community near where they really wanted to live is a better value that fits their realistic budget. When we engage in "possibility thinking," we can often find solutions we didn't see at first.

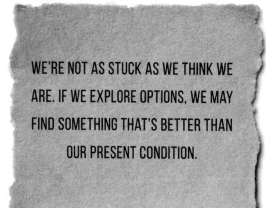

WE'RE NOT AS STUCK AS WE THINK WE ARE. IF WE EXPLORE OPTIONS, WE MAY FIND SOMETHING THAT'S BETTER THAN OUR PRESENT CONDITION.

Boredom, discouragement, and feeling out of place erode our enthusiasm and blunt our creativity. The good news is that we're not as stuck as we think we are. If we explore options, we may find something that's better than our present condition. The exploration itself, even if there's no change in the address, adds a measure of excitement to life. Failing to think, dream, and imagine makes us dull, and it usually leads to resentment, which then poisons every relationship. Don't be a victim. Don't settle for less. The pursuit will show you what you have control over—and it's almost certainly more than you think if you're in the pit of discouragement—and what is out of your hands, which is always significant. Instead of complaining about the things you can't control, take the initiative in the areas where you can make a difference.

I believe all of us should periodically ask the question of geography: "Why am I here?" Let me unpack this question by asking a few others:

+ Am I at the right company?

+ Am I investing in the right people?

+ Am I at my current place because I'm stuck and can't move?

+ Am I here because I've lost passion for impact?

+ Am I here because it's best for those I love, even though I pay a price?

+ Am I here because I have responsibilities to care for parents, grandchildren, or other family members?

+ Am I here because it's a very good place to invest my passion in the people I care about so I can fulfill our purpose?

I'm not suggesting this is a list you can check off the boxes and be done. We need to take time to think deeply so we can consider more than the binary options of stay or leave. Life is much more complex than that. We are complicated beings with a mixture of motives. The people we love need to know we're carefully considering the options. And at the end of our analytical process, we need to know we've been thorough.

We need to take the cap off our dreams so we can imagine a marvelous future, but we also must make a hard-nosed, pragmatic evaluation:

+ What role maximizes my education, talents, and training?

+ Where are the schools that are best for my children?

+ Where can we live where the housing and cost of living fit our budget?

+ Do we need or want to live close to parents or children?

+ Where is my network of friends?

+ If we move, how long will it take to cultivate new friendships? Is moving worth the emotional and relational cost of (probably) two years of feeling unsettled?

- ♦ Where can I invest some time in volunteering to serve?

- ♦ What's the tradeoff between the possibility of additional income and enjoying the people I work with?

- ♦ Who will I report to? Will a new boss be easier to work with?

- ♦ How long do I commute each day? How long would my commute take in another city?

Looking carefully at these factors can often tip the scales. Suddenly, we see our dreams from a different perspective. We may jump at a move even more eagerly, or we may realize things are much better than we thought right where we are. We belong here, after all. We're driving in the right lane.

FIVE DANGERS OF GETTING OUT OF YOUR LANE

When we're dissatisfied with our geography, we face a number of serious threats. These push us out of the lane where we can *"run with perseverance the race marked out for us"* (Hebrews 12:1) and they also may show that we're *already* out of our lane. Let me describe a few of them.

1. DISOBEDIENCE TO PRINCIPLES AND ETHICS

Boredom is the first symptom of feeling misplaced, but it's not the last. Soon, we take shortcuts in our work because it's not interesting and we don't care about excellence. Self-pity creeps into our thinking. We're sure we deserve better—in fact, we're entitled to a better job, a more agreeable board, a nicer boss, and a higher salary. We tell little lies to get out of trouble and eventually they become bigger lies. We avoid people and the truth so no one will ask too many questions. Does this scenario sound farfetched? It's much more common than you might think.

2. TERRITORIALISM

When we feel insecure about our place, we may guard our turf and resent anyone sticking their noses into our work. We don't freely share information because we don't want anyone to get ahead of us. We create a silo to keep others out and maintain complete control over our little kingdoms.

3. NEPOTISM

We may see people as for us or against us, so we favor a few and exclude all of the others. There's nothing inherently wrong with hiring family members—I've hired both of my daughters—but we cross a line when we make personnel decisions solely on personal loyalty without respect to competence, showing preference to the detriment of the organization. One of the most common critiques of insecure leaders is that they hire "yes" men and women.

4. INFLATED EGO

When leaders aren't sure of their place, some wilt and shrink, but others demand to be the center of attention. It's a coping strategy. They insist on receiving the credit for any success and they deflect any blame to those around them. They may have started their career as a servant leader instead of using people as stepping stones, but by this time, the only person who counts is the insecure leader. They spend every day proving they belong and they insist that everyone notice. Leaders who are confident of their place can relax, lead with grace, and affirm the contributions of others.

5. INSUBORDINATION

Leaders who have lost their sense of place feel isolated and they resent those above them on the organizational chart—and every leader reports to somebody, even if it's the board of directors or shareholders. Ironically, ambivalence can produce defiance and the leader senses opposition even when authority figures ask benign questions. When leaders no longer feel they belong, they live with an undercurrent of discouragement and anger. These emotions may be bottled up for a while, but sooner or later, the pressure builds. At the tipping point, one of two things happens: either the volcano explodes or the person implodes into depression. Neither is a pretty sight.

OTHERS MAY SEE THE PROBLEM FIRST

When we're in the wrong place, others can often tell before we notice the problem. Our spouse may ask, "Have you noticed that your temper is short these days? What's up with that?" A close friend might comment, "You don't seem to be excited about your work anymore. What's going on?" They might see us disengage or grumble more than usual. They may notice we're escaping into television or gaming. We haven't seen the symptoms, but they have. They see shifts that are imperceptible to us. For instance, we focus too much time and energy on people and projects that drain us, we don't care about much of anything anymore, we find fault in everything and everyone, every goal is a threat instead of a challenge, and everyone is against us.

When people find the courage to point out these things to us, we will almost certainly be resistant, at least at first. We don't want to believe the problem is us! We prefer to blame everyone else. But if we listen, we'll have the opportunity to learn, grow, and chart a new course for our careers... and maybe our lives.

IF WE'LL LISTEN, WE'LL HAVE THE OPPORTUNITY TO LEARN, GROW, AND CHART A NEW COURSE.

And if we're on the other side of the table from a person who feels out of place, we need equal measures of compassion and boldness as we speak the truth to our spouse, friend, child, or co-worker. We need to realize this is a hard message to hear, so we must speak with gentleness and grace. We probably don't understand what the underlying problem is; all we see are the surface symptoms. We just point out what we see and say, "Tell me what's going on with you." It will take time for the person to understand what led to this place of pain. Over many conversations, we listen. We don't insist on instant understanding and instant change. It took months or maybe years for the person to come to the painful conclusion he or she doesn't belong and it'll take time to rebuild confidence and find the right place again. With patience, persistence, and kindness, things will become clear.[16] The Danish philosopher

---

16. I recommend my book, *Leadership Pain*, for leaders who are struggling or for people who want to help those who are struggling. For more information about this book, see the resources section at the back of this book.

Søren Kierkegaard commented, "Life can only be understood backwards; but it must be lived forwards."

The challenge of geography isn't limited to those who are dissatisfied because growth has plateaued or the organization is declining. Sometimes, the most successful leaders have the itch to move.

I consulted with a pastor who planted a church in a community in the South and has seen it grow to over twelve thousand in attendance each week. He asked me to help him fulfill his dream of moving to a major city in the West to pastor a much smaller church there. He told me, "If God can use me to produce this church in this town, imagine how He might use me in that city!" He's convinced that his purpose can be fulfilled with passion for the people of that place. Restlessness had been building in his heart for years, but the timing wasn't right. Finally, when some pieces came together, he sensed it was time to make the move—no guarantees, but plenty of challenges to keep him on his toes. He had to weigh all the uncertainties, analyze the costs to himself and his family, and work through a comprehensive succession plan to leave his church in the hands of a gifted and wise leader.

I walked with him through this process. I never questioned his calling. It was obvious he had spent many hours thinking, praying, dreaming, and planning. I admired both his courage to go and his dedication to those who remained behind. I asked plenty of questions to help him plan more effectively. In addition to our conversations about his sense of calling to move, I asked what he would miss about his church and the people he was leaving. It was obvious he wasn't leaving because he was unhappy with them. He loved them deeply. I asked about the level of risk and his Plan B if the new church didn't work out like he hoped. He told me how his wife and children were processing the plan. My task was to take him to the edge of the cliff and let him see it clearly. If he still wanted to jump, it was entirely his decision. He jumped.

Many leaders don't even consider a move as dramatic as this pastor. Even minor changes in geography are too threatening. They're risk-averse, preferring safety to the problems inherent in any significant change of place. They doubt they have what it takes to make it anywhere else; besides, they're loyal to the people they serve and work with. They can't imagine living with the shame if their plans don't pan out—they interpret any career setback as a damning indictment of their character.

If the questions in this chapter have tweaked your heart, don't just turn the page and move on. Find someone you trust and share your thoughts, feelings, and desires. Look for a coach, a consultant, or someone in your profession who has no strings to your role. Give this person permission to ask you anything. When you answer, don't hedge and try to look like you've got it all together. Be ruthlessly honest about any sense that you don't fit or belong, that you're not in the right place anymore.

For some leaders, this chapter has identified some serious concerns and they need to start the process of evaluating their next move. They need to dig deep and find courage. Many other leaders will look at the points in this chapter and conclude their current place isn't perfect, but it's really good. They've lived with a low level of discontent, but now they're far more thankful they've found a good place. And I hope many leaders will realize they're in their sweet spot, right where they need to be. Excited, passionate leaders can help those around them evaluate their own geography and find the place where they belong. All of us need to answer the question of geography.

THINK ABOUT IT...

1. Have you ever felt like you're out of place, like you don't belong? If so, describe the situation and how it affected you.

2. How would you describe "the imposter syndrome"?

3. How clear and compelling are each of the four elements of your calling: purpose, passion, people, and place? Does one (or more) of them need attention? Explain your answer.

4. What are three or four of the most important questions in this chapter that you need to consider about your geography?

5. Have you noticed the "dangers of getting out of your lane" in people you've worked with? If so, what was the impact on the person and their relationships? Have you noticed these in your life? If you have, what's your next step?

6

WHAT TIME IS IT?
THE QUESTION OF MATURITY

> I insist on a lot of time being spent, almost every day,
> to just sit and think. That is very uncommon in American
> business. I read and think. So I do more reading and thinking,
> and make less impulse decisions than most people in business.
> I do it because I like this kind of life.
> —Warren Buffett

Comparison isn't always destructive. Sometimes, it gives us the opportunity to measure our progress and take steps forward. At least occasionally, as we look at ourselves in the mirror, we need to ask, *What should be happening in this season of my life? How should my thinking processes be better today than before? How can I tell if I'm making progress?*

I regularly ask myself these questions and I'm not always happy with the answers. I was raised in a pastor's home, surrounded by teaching from God's Word. I had the privilege to attend the best school in my city. I went to a very good college in the United States and earned my undergraduate and graduate degrees. I've pastored a church and I've seen lives changed. I've served as the president of a university. I've written books and, to some degree, every one of them has been designed to help leaders think more effectively. I've had the honor to consult with some of the finest, most respected leaders in the world. My life has been enriched and shaped by being a husband, father, and grandfather. I have wonderful friends who genuinely care about me. All of these things are unassailably true, but what in the world is operating in the recesses of my thinking when I get so angry as someone cuts me off in traffic? I want to give them the rude hand signal that does not mean, "You're number one."

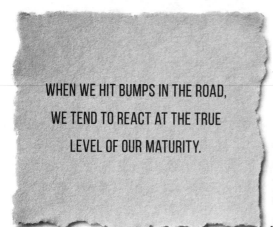

WHEN WE HIT BUMPS IN THE ROAD, WE TEND TO REACT AT THE TRUE LEVEL OF OUR MATURITY.

When the moment passes and I collect myself for a few minutes, I think, *Sam, with all of your education, all your training, all your experiences, and all the ways God has blessed you, why did those words come into your mind? No, you didn't say them out loud, but you wanted to. Why did you want to stop and punch that driver in the nose? How close to the surface is all that anger? It must be a powder keg waiting for a match. What's up with that kind of reaction? Shouldn't you be farther along than that? You're a preacher, a leader, a father, and grandfather. Don't you know better? Why haven't you matured so you don't have this kind of trigger on your anger?*

Maybe it's just me. Maybe I'm the only one who reverts to the reactions of a child when I experience unexpected disappointments.... No, I don't think so. When we hit bumps in the road, we tend to react at the true level of our maturity. That's a sobering and disheartening realization, but it's a pivot point for insight and growth.

The event on the highway isn't an isolated one. When I'm driving with Brenda in the car and she quickly points out that I'm about to hit someone, why do I seethe with contempt instead of saying, "Thank you, Dear. You saved our lives!" When I get poor service at a restaurant or the ticket agent at the airport is less than helpful, why do I shake my head in disgust instead of putting myself in their shoes? If someone else is asked to speak at an event, do I use a sour grapes excuse and insist I didn't want to go anyway?

I'm afraid there are many opportunities for self-reflection because there are many instances when my responses reveal the thinking of a child instead of a leader. I've spoiled too many meals, too many drives, too many conversations, and too many potentially wonderful moments because I've interpreted the people as fools and the events as threats. No grace, no compassion, no wisdom. Yes, it hurts to admit it, but it's necessary to be honest, first with myself, then with Brenda, and now with you.

Like most of us, I'm careful to avoid letting my guard down when I'm in the spotlight. No matter how upset I am inside, I'm cool and calm on the outside. The true level of my maturity and an accurate picture of my thinking shows up in the unguarded moments, especially with my family, in the car, or when I'm traveling. If I speak at an event and some person on the back row is critical of my talk, it doesn't bother me. If one of my church elders voices criticism, it matters more. If the pastor or Brenda pulls me aside to point out my errors or omissions, it hurts far more. The level of pain—and defensiveness—rises with the proximity of the other person.

Don't leave me hanging here! Let me ask you: Who gets your goat? When do you react with contempt? What recurring circumstances bring out flashes of defensiveness? When are you more like a child than a mature leader? (Now you can share my pain.)

We make a great mistake when we equate business or organizational success with personal maturity. I know some leaders who have achieved magnificent success, but emotionally and relationally, they are as fragile as teenagers.

UNDERSTAND YOUR SEASON

Too often, we react with immaturity because we don't anticipate possible difficulties. Some problems happen when we don't expect them, like on the highway, although I'd argue that I should have learned to expect drivers to cut me off occasionally. But many of the stress-producing situations in our lives are observable, repeatable, and seasonal. Even the best seed planted in the wrong season will die. In the same way, leaders need to understand their current season.

We sometimes experience seasons of great harvest, but those are episodic, not continual. They come after seasons of fallow ground in winter, when we see the first signs of growth in an organization's spring and we've endured long periods of hard labor to prepare for harvest.

We are well aware of seasons in retail and church life. Many stores have half their annual sales between Black Friday after Thanksgiving and Christmas Day. They plan sales to take advantage of particular seasons to entice people to come to their stores or go online to buy. These companies order products months ahead and they hire a flock of extra people to be ready for the rush of shoppers. The seasons of planning and preparation are just as important as the brief time when the cash registers are ringing and credit cards are sliding.

Churches gear up for Christmas and Easter, but aren't idle the rest of the year. They're building leaders, crafting programs, and preparing for the people who only walk through the doors a couple of times a year. Attendance often rises at the start of the school year and the beginning of the New Year. Wise leaders are prepared to capture those moments when hearts are particularly open.

Marriages have fairly predictable seasons of bliss and doubt, building strength through deeper communication and having that bond tested by in-laws, children, money, and differences in sexual appetites. These four issues probably constitute 90 percent of the conversations of couples in therapy. Ignoring the differences guarantees that when conflict happens, it will be even more intense. Instead, a focused season of honesty, vulnerability, and compromise can take the couple to a new season of understanding and joy.

The political cycle is two or four years and the parties invest countless hours and endless sums of money to prepare to win votes. We used to focus our attention on the voting process only a few months before elections, but now it appears we're always in election season.

Some new mothers choose to spend a season at home with infants and little children. They may have had blossoming careers, but they've made a financial, relational decision to adjust their careers for a different pursuit. When the kids are a little older and the family is in a different season, mom will probably decide to reengage her career. Young fathers may not have as much time for sports and friends as they devote more time at home. Someday, the season of sports will probably return, but it may be a less strenuous endeavor, like bowling instead of basketball.

THE SEASONS IN A LEADER'S LIFE

We can identify broad seasons that characterize the lives of most leaders:

FIRST ATTEMPTS

In the early years, they try a lot of things to see what roles fit their passions and talents. In past generations, people often had limited choices—they worked in the same jobs as their fathers and grandfathers. Today, young people have an almost limitless array of possibilities, which is both thrilling and perplexing to many of them.

THE SWEET SPOT

At some point, most leaders find the sweet spot and they devote themselves to learning, growing, and excelling in their chosen field. They may go back to school, seek on-the-job training, or create a new business in their garage. In this season, the rising leader is honing skills and developing confidence.

RUNNING HARD

Virtually all leaders have an extended season of running long and hard, reaching higher, refining their leadership skills, and gaining insights about themselves and those around them. They realize there are particular seasons in their families, their own lives, and their companies, and they take advantages of those times.

MENTORING

In later years, leaders have more wisdom than energy, so their season shifts to be more of an advisor than the one who implements the plans. This doesn't devalue the leader's influence. In fact, this may be a season for greater impact than ever before.

I've noticed a turning point in the lives of leaders: before they are about forty-five years old, they get ahead by saying "yes." After that time, they advance by learning to say "no." In the earlier season, they're eager to try new things and take bigger risks—and they're often afraid to say "no" when asked to do something. But in the later season, they're more focused, more interested in doing a few things well than trying to do everything. And they have more confidence, so they can more easily say "no," even to good opportunities.

I first noticed this pattern in my own life. For me, the turning point came when I was about forty-eight. Before then, I said "yes" when anyone asked me to speak—at churches, civic meetings, and even to women's groups and children's church. "You want me to speak at all five services? No problem, I'll be glad to." I didn't have a "no" muscle because I never exercised it. In fact, the idea of saying "no" to anyone created a lot of anxiety in me. I wondered, *If I say "no" this time, will anyone ever ask me again?* Saying "no" meant I missed the immediate opportunity, but I also risked future opportunities. As I became a consultant, I took on everyone who asked me. I didn't realize that having two high-paying clients was better than having ten who couldn't really afford me.

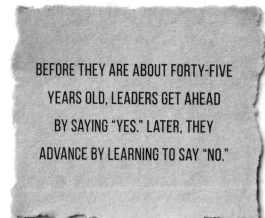

BEFORE THEY ARE ABOUT FORTY-FIVE YEARS OLD, LEADERS GET AHEAD BY SAYING "YES." LATER, THEY ADVANCE BY LEARNING TO SAY "NO."

My thinking changed at that critical season. I realized I was limiting myself—and exhausting myself—by always saying "yes." A new thought formed in my mind: I had to give up to go up. I had to say "no" broadly so I could say "yes" selectively. Since that time, I've turned down far more opportunities than I've taken. I've more carefully identified my zone of effectiveness—to influence influencers—and I make decisions to stay there. The fear that I experienced before has subsided because I'm more confident this is the right path for me.

The importance of using "no" to focus my attention on a select audience was confirmed when I took twenty-two top leaders to Panama to speak to them on the principles from my book, *Bigger, Faster Leadership*. The book uses the construction of the Panama Canal as a metaphor and a template for building organizations. In the first meeting, I gave each one a piece of paper and asked them to write down the organizations they influence and the size of each one. Between meetings, I asked someone to calculate the total. I announced to the group that this small number of leaders influenced more than fourteen million people. In influencing them, I'm definitely in my zone. I've learned to always ask every audience or individual, "What's next? What journey are we on together to have a greater impact?" This question is now at the heart of my purpose.

In the early seasons of our leadership careers, we pursue certainty and we feel uncomfortable with ambiguity. After a certain point, however, perhaps when we learn to say "no," we realize the best leaders aren't threatened when they don't know the answers and can't make instant decisions.

I believe Moses was a higher-level leader than Joshua. The younger man had been to the Promised Land as a spy. His thinking was crisp and clear; his purpose was focused like a laser. Moses, on the other hand, moved the people only when the pillar of fire or smoke moved, not on his command. He had to deal with devastating shortages of food and water, rebellion, criticism, and personal heartache. Through all the complexity and confusion, he became one of the most outstanding leaders the world has ever known. Do we insist on certainty and clear decisions within a prescribed timeframe? If we do, we may be very good generals like Joshua, but we may not be a great leader like Moses.

THE NECESSITY OF DISRUPTION

Good leaders may feel successful when they dot all the I's and cross all the T's, but great leaders understand that their lives and their leadership are inherently disruptive. They are thinking new thoughts, introducing new ideas, charting new paths, creating new products and services, finding new ways to connect with people, and, in all of this, creating a lot of tension before they resolve any of it. MBA professor and corporate culture expert John Mattone observes, "The comfort zone—yes, it feels good, but in reality is the most painful existence and is not going to get you anywhere. The best CEOs are constantly disruptive."[17]

We don't create disruption as a means of throwing people off balance so we can control them. That's pathology, not leadership. Instead, we understand that a certain level of disturbance is inevitable as we move our organizations forward. King Solomon may not have been a farmer or a rancher, but he understood how to use analogies from the countryside. He wrote, "*Where there are no oxen, the manger is clean, but abundant crops come by the strength of the ox*" (Proverbs 14:4 ESV). If we want everything in our organizations to be neat and clean, we'll miss out on the opportunity to use the creativity and strength of our brightest people—people whose contributions often create messes!

We have the responsibility to create a certain level of disruption by intentionally enlisting the best ideas and trying new directions. Otherwise, we will suffer disruption forced upon us by circumstances that seem beyond our control. Either we will lead boldly in the midst of disruption or it will crush us—it's our choice. Leaders who insist on a consistent, predictable environment value safety above progress and their goal is to avoid losing. Many of our people prefer a predictable environment, but we know the value of "guided disruption." Our task is to help our people see the benefits in the seasons of ambiguity when things aren't clear, the seasons of chaos when the end isn't in sight, and the seasons of doubt when they wonder if we've lost our minds. These are the disruptive times when great advances can occur. They are the seasons of possibility, hope, and exponential growth.

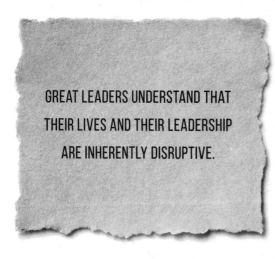

GREAT LEADERS UNDERSTAND THAT THEIR LIVES AND THEIR LEADERSHIP ARE INHERENTLY DISRUPTIVE.

---

17. John Mattone, speaking at The World Business Forum, cited in *CEO Magazine*, May 2016, http://updates.theceomagazine.com/hubfs/2016/September/Articles/PDFs_/CEO_AU_SEP16_WBF.pdf?t=1471584735655.

I hope I'm disrupting your thinking. I want to push you to think about embracing the seasons of ambiguity and even welcoming them instead of believing there's something tragically wrong when you don't have all the answers. I want to make you feel uncomfortable…and like it! In fact, if you don't feel resistant to this concept, I haven't pushed hard enough.

I want you to think of me as a dentist and you're in the chair. The closer I get to you and the exposed nerve with the drill in my hand, the more you squirm. If you get up and leave, you'll still have that cavity and it will cause more harm. But if you overcome your resistance, stay in the chair, and give yourself to the process, we can address the problem so you can move on with your life.

Another analogy makes the same point: a fighter pilot knows he's in the right spot when he's getting anti-aircraft fire. If you're not catching flack for your disruptive ideas, you're not over your target yet. Keep flying.

Let me press a little more: Newton's third law says that every action has an equal and opposite reaction. If your goal is to eliminate all disruption, you won't move at all. If you move, if you rock the boat and make waves, you'll get an equal and opposite reaction, at least from some people. Sometimes the resistance is your own sense that good leadership should create a smooth pond; this idea

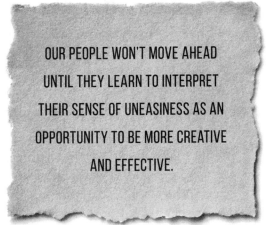

OUR PEOPLE WON'T MOVE AHEAD UNTIL THEY LEARN TO INTERPRET THEIR SENSE OF UNEASINESS AS AN OPPORTUNITY TO BE MORE CREATIVE AND EFFECTIVE.

of disruptive leadership seems foreign, strange, and wrong. But often, the resistance comes from those who expect you to always give them smooth waters. Your job is to help them embrace disruption and ambiguity so real progress can happen.

Counselors, coaches, and great business leaders understand that resistance is unavoidable if organizations are going to move forward. It's not a flaw and it's not a sin. We don't make progress personally without creating tension between what has been and what can be. The people in our organizations won't move ahead until they learn to interpret their sense of uneasiness as an opportunity to be more creative and effective than ever. Our job is to reframe their resistance for them.

I'm not saying that every time others resist our ideas that we're right and they're slow and dense. They may have very good reasons to resist our ideas! Resistance forces us to think more deeply, communicate more clearly, determine if the path we're on can be improved, and then help people see the benefits of a season of chaos.

WHY CHANGE IS SO HARD

Some processes in nature are clear and direct: we plant an apple tree and if we care for it, we'll get apples in the fall; if we have a drainage problem, we can dig a ditch to drain the water away. So why is it so hard for people to change, even those who are leaders and are dedicated to leading change in their organizations?

Pastor Charles Stone has made some remarkable observations about resistance to change, resistance that is rooted deep in the gray cells and synapses of our brains. If we understand the inner workings of our brains, we won't be so surprised when we or others are so slow to do the very things that promise life, health, growth, and success.

Stone taps into research showing that two-thirds of the cells in our amygdala, the most basic part of our brains, are wired for freeze, fight, or flight. We pick up negative signals from our environment more readily than positive ones, so we're normally and continually on guard. When this part of the brain is activated, people respond naturally with fear, which triggers the defensive reactions.

Preexisting emotions and perceptions are like a door in our brains that is open or closed to change. People who are already fearful, anxious, hurt, or ashamed have barricades over the door, shutting off any opportunity to change course and take courageous steps forward. No matter how many "convincing facts" the leader presents, the barricade effectively keeps the door closed.

Resistance to change becomes more acute as the event approaches. When the change was in the distant future, people may be open and even eager because it's still just a concept. However, as the moment of implementation draws near, anxiety rises, fears multiply, and our minds run on overdrive imagining the costs more than the benefits. At this point, people ask more questions, but often to find a way out, not to move ahead. Stone observes, "Uninformed optimism gives way to informed pessimism."[18]

As we age, the wiring in our brains becomes more rigid, so we're less open to change. The caricature of the grumpy old man who refuses to consider even the slightest positive change has more than a grain of truth to it. We gradually become more fixed in our thinking and established habits of a lifetime make it difficult to consider new possibilities.

Our brains produce several chemicals that heighten our sense of happiness, contentment, and pleasure: dopamine, oxytocin, serotonin, and endorphins. We naturally move toward activities that release these chemicals and we naturally move away from those that block them. Our brains usually interpret change as a threat, which blocks these chemicals, and our brains interpret the opportunity to escape from change as a signal to release them.

Thus, resistance to change is not clearly reasoned and carefully considered. It's the brain's way of warning us that change might be dangerous. We can overcome this natural freeze, fight, or flight reaction by creating an environment where people feel safe and appreciated, releasing the positive chemicals in the brain, which then opens the door to talk about the benefits of change. Speak not only to the people sitting in front of you; speak to the inner workings of their brains.[19]

THE TASK OF REFRAMING

I've seen plenty of people who endured long seasons of discouragement, even depression, because they didn't know how to reframe failure or heartache. The painful events consumed their thinking and soon eradicated all the joy in their lives. In this negative, discouraging mind-set, even great success gave them no more than momentary relief. They were in a long winter of discontent, but without hope of spring.

---

18. Charles Stone, *Brain-Savvy Leaders: The Science of Significant Ministry* (Nashville, TN: Abingdon Press, 2015), 145.
19. Charles Stone, "8 Neurological Reasons Why Church Change Is So Difficult," *Outreach Magazine*, March 5, 2018, http://www.outreachmagazine.com/features/leadership/27000-8-neurological-reasons-church-change-difficult.html.

When we're in a season of hard times, it's easy to lose perspective. We need to do something that is the opposite of our natural inclination—we want to isolate and hide, but instead we need to find a couple of people who will walk through it with us. We need people who exhibit three vital characteristics: competence, candor, and commitment. They need to be experienced and skilled in helping people who are struggling. We don't call Uncle Harold because he's the only one we can think of. We make a short list of people who have a track record of providing true wisdom. We look for people who will tell us the truth—the positive truth about our strengths and God's love, but also the hard truth of where we've drifted off true north. And we need people who are committed to us even when we're resistant, even when we avoid them, and even when we're so slow to change. These are people who, as one leader described them, always let us in but never let us down.

> WE CAN'T MOVE FORWARD UNTIL WE GRIEVE WHAT WE COULDN'T CONTROL, FORGIVE THOSE WHO WRONGED US, AND ASK FOR FORGIVENESS FOR THE WRONGS WE'VE COMMITTED.

Many people in this dark season feel overwhelmed by stress. Sometimes, the pressure and loss happened in a flash, but more often, it accrued slowly… so slowly the leader didn't notice until the damage was done. Stress is the perception of helplessness in dealing with serious demands. It doesn't exist in isolation; it's always the product of difficulties with people and events. The response to those difficulties depends on the leader's sense of adequacy to deal with them. That's why some leaders become stronger by going through hard times and others falter. Popular culture says the answer is to retreat, escape, and avoid the stress. That may be helpful for a temporary respite, but it won't address the underlying problem. Leaders need to think better so they can act better and then, sooner or later, they'll probably feel better.

Losses are a fact of life. As long as we're above ground, we'll suffer heartaches, betrayal, and failure of one kind or another. One of our challenges is to accurately assign responsibility. Many people feel guilty over things they didn't control and many deny responsibility for wrongs they committed. We can't move forward until we sort these things out, grieve what we couldn't control, forgive those who wronged us, and ask for forgiveness for the wrongs we've committed. We're all deeply flawed, but we can have a new identity as God's loved, forgiven, and adopted children. As Winston Churchill said, "We are all worms, but I do believe I am a glow worm."

If we look hard enough, we'll realize there is redemptive value in every failure—whoever caused it. If we learn to think rightly about it, we'll have realistic expectations, we'll learn to see stresses through a hopeful lens, and we'll live with more peace and security. This will give us the platform to help those around us reframe the seasons of difficulty they endure. Those we view as heroes today aren't considered great because of unbroken success, but because they overcame crushing failure and adversity.

MY SEASONS, YOUR SEASONS

Life is anything but static. Reflecting on his marriage, theologian Lewis Smedes wrote:

> When I married my wife, I had hardly a smidgen of sense for what I was getting into with her. How could I know how much she would change over 25 years? How could I know how much I would change? My wife has lived with at least five different men since we were wed—and each of the five has been me.[20]

Like Smedes, I've had more seasons than a television show and Brenda has patiently been with me through all of them. Each time—whether I was a student, a youth pastor, a senior pastor, a university president, or a consultant—I tried to understand the expectations so my thoughts, words, and actions were appropriate for that season of my life. I wasn't thinking about the next season. I just wanted to be mature in that season.

Some of us are aspirational leaders; we have carefully constructed plans to move ahead in our careers. I'm an accidental leader; all the changes in my role over the years were a surprise to me. Actually, the

---

20. Lewis Smedes, "Controlling the Unpredictable—The Power of Promising," *Christianity Today*, January 21, 1983, 16–19.

one aspiration I had was to be a pastor because my father was a pastor, but all the rest of these roles were thrust upon me. Perhaps the most unusual was becoming president of the university. The bylaws of the school required them to select someone who was a member of the denomination and had a graduate degree. I was one of three people who qualified for the post and the other two weren't interested in the job. That left me as the only viable candidate. I guess the board's meeting wasn't too contentious.

Each of these seasons required me to grow, develop, and learn to think better than before.

I sometimes have conversations with people who say, "Sam, I'd like to do what you do. What steps can I take?"

I respond, "That's great. Just put yourself in a position to learn and share what you've learned."

I don't say, "You know, you're only twenty-seven years old. You're just figuring out what you want to do. You don't have enough experience and wisdom yet. Live a little, lead a lot, and see where it takes you. You need to look like you're wise. Come back in twenty or thirty years and we'll talk more about it."

WE'RE MATURE AND GAINING WISDOM WHEN...

We don't necessarily become mature with advancing birthdays. I know some young people who are mature far beyond their years and I know some older people who act like children. I know because I'm sometimes one of them. How do we know we're gaining wisdom? Here are some indications:

WE LISTEN TO PEOPLE WHO HOLD DIFFERENT VIEWS

This includes people with political persuasions, business philosophies, leadership goals, and theological perspectives that are different than ours. We don't have to agree with them and we don't need to buy what they're selling, but we can show the respect of an open ear. To find out more, we ask second and third questions. We learn and grow when we're exposed to people who have different perspectives. All growth is about exposure.

WE LOVE PEOPLE WHO AREN'T VERY LOVABLE

Who do you think of when you read that sentence? Virtually all of us have faces flash in front of us. Yes, we can love them, but everybody is unlovable at one time or another—even you and me.

WE REALIZE WE NEED TO SUBMIT TO OTHERS' LEADERSHIP

We won't mature in wisdom and strength on our own. We need to follow a leader so we can absorb the lessons they have learned. Business leaders often recognize the importance of a mentor and they attend conferences to sharpen their thinking. Pastors too often try to lead alone. Everyone needs a coach or mentor—no exceptions. It doesn't have to be someone in town, in the same field, or in the same faith tradition, but it must be someone who has earned our respect so we are willing to be open and honest.

WE REFRAME STRESS AND FAILURE SO WE CAN LEARN FROM THESE TIMES

Our perceptions of success and failure are downloaded in our brains from the time we're small children. They don't change easily, but they can certainly change. As we've seen, learning to reframe adversity is one of the most important things leaders will ever do. It will radically affect their attitudes, their relationships, their passion, and their health.

WE THINK MORE EXPANSIVELY AND ASK BETTER QUESTIONS

Immature people are thinking about what they're going to say while others are talking, but a mature person is fully present, seeking to understand before seeking to be understood. We are no longer "locked in" to a single way to see a person, an opportunity, a problem, or an event. We ask plenty of questions and over time, our questions become more incisive. We spend time with people who have very different experiences and perspectives instead of only hanging out with people who agree with us about virtually everything.

When was the last time you were in an uncomfortable conversation? What about it made you feel uncomfortable? Did you run away, fight back, or slow down and engage the person more fully?

WE NEVER STOP FOLLOWING OUR DREAMS

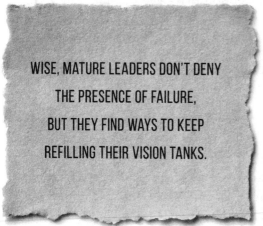

WISE, MATURE LEADERS DON'T DENY THE PRESENCE OF FAILURE, BUT THEY FIND WAYS TO KEEP REFILLING THEIR VISION TANKS.

We often begin our tenure as leaders full of vision and enthusiasm, but over time, we can lose heart. Many leaders I meet think back on "the good old days" before the stresses and strains began to take a heavy toll on them. Wise, mature leaders don't deny the presence of failure and countless other difficulties, but they find ways to keep refilling their vision tanks. They're not surprised when the level of their passion and enthusiasm goes down; it's a fact of life. But they're always reading great books and articles, listening to podcasts, and talking to other leaders to stay filled and overflowing.

All of us have room to grow, to learn, and to mature a bit more—maybe a lot more. I appreciate men and women who have the courage to admit they're still in process and, in fact, they'll always be in process. They recognize the seasons on the calendar, but even more, they notice the seasons in their own lives. Thinking through the seasons of life gives them perspective, patience, and hope.

THINK ABOUT IT...

1. What irritates you? What events or people cause you to revert to a childish response? (If you're sitting next to someone on your list, write in code!)

2. How would you characterize the season of life you're in right now? What season is your family in? How does it help to recognize the opportunities and limitations of the seasons?

3. What are some benefits of saying "yes" when you're young? Why is it important to develop a "no" muscle at some point? Are you at that point yet? Why or why not?

4. Do you naturally embrace or resist the need to be a disruptive leader? Explain your answer.

5. What are some common ways most people interpret failure and difficulties? How do these interpretations affect them and those around them?

6. What are some ways it would help you to reframe hardships? What difference will it make?

7. Who can you trust to help you navigate the current and next seasons of your life?

7

WHO WILL JOIN ME?
THE QUESTION OF TEAM

Never worry alone. When anxiety grabs my mind, it is self-
perpetuating. Worrisome thoughts reproduce faster than rabbits,
so one of the most powerful ways to stop the spiral of worry is
simply to disclose my worry to a friend....
The simple act of reassurance from another human being
[becomes] a tool of the Spirit to cast out fear—because
peace and fear are both contagious.
—John Ortberg, Jr.

In 2004, the Summer Olympic Games returned to Greece, the site of
the original games over 2,500 years ago. The United States took the finest
athletes from our nation to compete in dozens of sports. For the previous
two Summer Games, our basketball teams hadn't been the best *amateurs*
in the country; they were the best *professional* players from the National
Basketball Association. The 2004 "dream team" had a host of future Hall
of Fame stars, including LeBron James, Dwayne Wade, Tim Duncan, and
Allen Iverson, and they were led by Hall of Fame coach Larry Brown. Of
all the basketball teams the world had ever assembled, this one would have

ranked at or near the top. Everyone, even the players on other teams, considered them unbeatable.

They weren't. In the first game, the United States played the small Caribbean commonwealth of Puerto Rico. It was to be just a warm-up for the U.S., but the unknown players from Puerto Rico blew the professionals out of the gym. The final score was a totally embarrassing 92 to 73, the worst loss (and only the third loss) in U.S. Olympic basketball history. Brown and the players insisted it was only a wake-up call.

The U.S. team labored to win the next two games against Greece and Australia. They then faced the tiny Baltic country of Lithuania. In another stunning loss, the U.S. was defeated 94 to 90. Now they faced an uphill fight for a gold medal. They defeated two more teams, Angola and Spain. In the semifinals, they faced a surprisingly strong squad from Argentina. The South Americans outplayed the mighty Americans and won 89 to 81. The U.S. played Lithuania again in a consolation game for the bronze medal. This time, they won, but the sting of defeat couldn't be erased. The dream team that had traveled to Greece with such high expectations left as the nightmare team. Larry Brown took responsibility for the poor teamwork, saying:

> I'm humiliated, not for the loss—I can always deal with wins and losses—but I'm disappointed because I had a job to do as a coach, to get us to understand how we're supposed to play as a team and act as a team, and I don't think we did that.[21]

A DIFFERENT TEAM AND OUTCOME

Another set of athletes can tell a very different story about teamwork. Joe Rantz grew up about as poor as anyone could be during the Great Depression. His future looked bleak, but he had two assets: he was an incredible athlete and he had a strong drive to succeed. He did well in school and he earned a scholarship to the University of Washington. There, he tried out for the eight-man rowing team. His talent was raw, but the coach was impressed with Joe's grit and determination. Joe made the team and over two years, he settled into a crew with seven other young

---

21. "Ugly American Basketball," Thomas S. Hibbs, *National Review*, August 16, 2004, https://www.nationalreview.com/2004/08/ugly-american-basketball-thomas-s-hibbs.

men who in 1935 were determined to beat their long-time nemesis, the University of California at Berkeley. In a stirring race, Washington won. They traveled east to race against the best rowers in the Ivy League and, surprisingly, they won there, too. Their goal, though, wasn't only to beat college teams in America. The 1936 Olympic Games in Berlin were on the horizon and they wanted to qualify as America's entry. The next year, they beat the best in America and they qualified for the games in Berlin.

When they arrived in Germany, the eight rowers and their feisty coxswain, Bobby Moch, didn't have impressive credentials. They were the sons of shipyard workers, loggers, and farmers—but they had beaten the sons of bankers, lawyers, business barons, and senators. Now they faced the golden-haired sons of the Nazi elite. On the day of the race in Berlin, the Americans were assigned an outside lane that exposed them to a strong headwind. The Germans got the preferred inside lane and were heavy favorites, especially since Adolf Hitler showed up to watch the race. For most of the course, the Americans were behind. Then, in one of the most stunning upsets in Olympic history, the U.S. team came from nowhere to edge out the Germans at the finish line. It happened because nine young men believed in each other, pulled for each other, and gave everything they had for each other. Daniel James Brown's stirring account of this team, *The Boys in the Boat*, gives vivid details of how this team achieved what most thought was impossible. Brown comments:

> Against the grim backdrop of the Great Depression, they reaffirmed the American notion that merit, in the end, outweighs birthright. They reminded the country of what can be done when everyone quite literally pulls together. And they provided hope that in the titanic struggle that lay just ahead, the ruthless might of the Nazis would not prevail over American grit, determination, and optimism.[22]

As I've analyzed businesses, nonprofit organizations, and churches, I've seen it again and again: thoroughly average people who work as a team will surpass incredibly talented people who don't pull together as a team. On the way to success, teamwork trumps talent.

22. From the author's website, *The Boys in the Boat*, Daniel James Brown, http://www.danieljamesbrown.com/books/the-boys-in-the-boat/#.WuCXjsgh1-0.

LESSONS FROM THE ROWING TEAM

The young men on that University of Washington rowing team can teach us valuable lessons about how teams function most effectively. Let me make a few observations:

EVERYONE MUST FACE IN THE SAME DIRECTION

Think about how ridiculous it would look if several of the men in the boat tried to row in the opposite direction. There would be chaos and conflict, the boat wouldn't move much at all, and they'd have no chance of winning a race. On our teams, everyone needs to be crystal clear about the finish line so everyone is expending effort to go in the same direction.

THE COXSWAIN PACES THE TEAM FOR THE LONG HAUL

The coxswain—the onboard, de facto coach—sets the pace and direction, executes strategy, and facilitates communication between the rowers. If the team goes out too fast, they won't have enough energy left for the sprint to the finish line. The coxswain sets the rhythm for the rowers' strokes, watching the wind and the other boats, to know when to ask for maximum effort.

EACH ROWER MAINTAINS PERSONAL DISCIPLINE

Rowing requires incredible strength and endurance over the course of the race. Taking the oar out too fast or too slow, catching water on the return, or failing to keep the exact pace set by the coxswain slows down the boat and can cause oars to clash, possibly preventing the team from winning. Each person on the team has to maintain rigorous disciple from start to finish.

EACH PERSON HAS A PARTICULAR RESPONSIBILITY

One or two members of the team are counted on for strength. When others are tired, these people pull even harder. Others have the role of being smooth and methodical in their strokes. One person near the coxswain is the one the others look to for the pace. This rower sets the example for all the others to follow.

THE RACE IS AGAINST YOUR BEST TIME

Certainly, you want to beat the other boats on the water, but beating your best time is the best goal for a rowing team. If the coxswain feels the need to always be out front, he'll start with a pace the team can't keep up and they'll fade in the middle or by the end of the race. Each team needs to find the pace and rhythm that brings out their best.

THE COXSWAIN IS THE CAPTAIN OF THE BOAT

All the rowers have their backs to the finish line. They can't see where they're going, but they see the coxswain sitting in the back of the boat with one hand on the rudder and the other hand on the megaphone to shout directions. From countless hours together in practice and in races, they've learned to trust his instructions, even when it seems they're falling too far behind.

TEAMWORK RESULTS IN FUN

Among the young men on the Washington team, competition was a way of life, but it was friendly competition. They pushed each other to try harder, to be more disciplined, and to work together more fully. As they saw progress, they celebrated each second they knocked off their best time. And with each practice and race, they grew to love and respect each other even more.

ON THE WAY TO SUCCESS, TEAMWORK TRUMPS TALENT.

Do these lessons apply to you and your team? Of course they do.

CULTURE STARTS AT THE TOP

Mid-level managers, staff members, frontline employees, and volunteers don't establish the culture of an organization, but their attitudes and actions are vivid evidence of the culture. No matter how many times the CEO proclaims, "We're a customer-focused company," it doesn't take too many poor service experiences with grumpy salespeople to reveal that statement is false. When we return a shirt that didn't fit or a wrench we don't need, the look on the clerk's face tells us volumes about the company's environment and values.

In my book, *Culture Catalyst*, I describe a range of cultures from healthy to unhealthy. An organization's culture can be inspiring, accepting, stagnant, discouraging, or toxic. To summarize the characteristics of each one:

+   In *inspiring* cultures, leaders cultivate an atmosphere of trust and respect, creativity is rewarded, and failures are viewed as stepping stones of growth.

+   In *accepting* cultures, the atmosphere is generally positive, but people have to walk on eggshells about certain topics. Leaders invest in developing people, but they are often too slow to make necessary changes in personnel.

+   In *stagnant* cultures, staff members are seen as units of production, not as valued people. Employees tolerate their leaders, but they have little respect for them. Complaining becomes the most popular sport and people are more concerned about their paychecks and status than the company's vision.

+   In *discouraging* cultures, the executives care only about their prestige, power, and purses. Power struggles are a daily game and survival is the daily goal for employees. In this environment, the leaders become more rigid and demanding. The culture is created at the top, sustained at the bottom, and grown or destroyed in the middle.

+   In *toxic* cultures, leaders abuse their power at the expense of everyone in the organization. Fear is the most common motivation among the staff. Ethical lapses are ignored. These organizations run off their best people and attract only those who are desperate or foolish enough to join the chaos.[23]

---

23. Condensed and adapted from *Culture Catalyst*, Samuel R. Chand (New Kensington, PA: Whitaker House, 2018), 27–39.

TAKE A HARD LOOK

How can leaders evaluate the health of their organization's culture? Too often, we're so close to the people and processes that we don't have a clear perspective. One of the ways to look at any environment is to compare it to a set of benchmarks. Review this list of common symptoms of an unhealthy culture:

+ The frontline employees and volunteers lack enthusiasm. They complain more than they celebrate.

+ Passionate, visionary conversations among the staff are rare. Why is this important? The topic of our conversations is often what's most important to us. When we don't talk about our hopes and dreams, it may indicate these have died.

+ There is a high turnover rate among employees and volunteers.

+ We spend an inordinate amount of time trying to resolve misunderstandings and conflicts.

+ People form cliques and these groups alienate and resent each other.

+ "Office politics" and power struggles are a constant drain on time and attention.

+ When people laugh, it's at sarcasm.

+ Mid-level leaders protect their turf and create silos so no one can tell them what to do.

+ Success creates as much resentment as celebration.

+ The work load isn't smooth and predictable. Unrealistic deadlines and a frenetic rush of work is followed by awkward and confusing lulls.

+ Gossip poisons the atmosphere and makes people vicious or self-protective...or both.

+ Leaders let all of this happen without having the wisdom or the courage to address it.

(If you want the people in your organization to take a free survey to measure seven characteristics of culture, go to www.samchandculturesurvey.com.)

Every organization has a distinct culture. A stagnant, discouraging, or toxic culture creates a cloud of suspicion, distrust, and fear. Great leaders—leaders who notice and think about the culture of their teams—take responsibility to create a healthy environment in which people feel valued and want to give their best each day.

Culture is more important than strategy. Peter Drucker comments, "Culture eats strategy for breakfast."[24] And I say, a toxic culture eats vision for lunch.

THREE CULTURAL "MUSTS"

From my experience with leaders in a wide range of organizations, I've identified three factors that are crucial to happiness, teamwork, and productivity:

1. POSITIVE FEEDBACK

In healthy organizations, leaders give frequent and genuine affirmation. They're looking for opportunities to pat people on the back, point out creativity and tenacity to get the job done, and steps of success. They speak these words of encouragement publicly as well as privately, making "deposits" in each person's emotional bank account. In this environment, "withdrawals" of correction don't drain the account dry.

2. MUTUAL RESPECT

In positive, productive cultures, leaders cultivate passion in their people so they can get buy-in by suggesting and requesting—inviting people to take the initiative to find creative ways to accomplish a task—rather than demanding compliance. These leaders take time to listen; they ask for input and feedback in a collaborative relationship. Instead of always being the source of "the right answer," they often ask others, "What do you think we should do?" "What are your best ideas?" "What do you think is our next step?" Respect brings out the best in people. John Mattone, an expert in company culture, states, "The role of the CEO nowadays is to

---

24. Cited in "Drucker Said 'Culture Eats Strategy for Breakfast' And Enterprise Rent-A-Car Proves It," Shep Hyken, *Forbes*, December 5, 2015, https://www.forbes.com/sites/shephyken/2015/12/05/drucker-said-culture-eats-strategy-for-breakfast-and-enterprise-rent-a-car-proves-it/#7d099ba22749.

create a culture that unleashes people, and it is the most important job that exists."[25] They are the CCOs: chief culture officers.

3. CONNECTION TO A HIGHER PURPOSE

Great leaders focus on the "why" before they articulate the "what." In an inspiring culture, every person—from the executive team to the greeters or those who work in the call center—understands that what they do each day is accomplishing something far bigger and more valuable than checking tasks off a list or making money. These leaders continually remind people throughout the organization of the big picture; in fact, they become masters at articulating this vision in fresh, meaningful ways.

Don't assume you're doing a great job in these three critical areas. Have the courage to think more clearly. Take the time to look at the culture you're creating, ask some honest people for their feedback on these areas, and take steps to excel still more in these important factors of creating a great team.

LEADERS AND LADDERS

For years, I've used the analogy of climbing ladders to represent a leader's upward mobility. The point is that we can only climb as high as the strength and skill of those who are holding our ladders. If we've chosen and developed only those who are moderately strong and talented, we can only use a ladder that goes up ten feet. If we have people who have greater abilities, we can use a twenty-foot ladder.

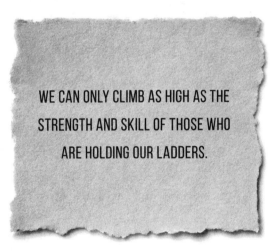

WE CAN ONLY CLIMB AS HIGH AS THE STRENGTH AND SKILL OF THOSE WHO ARE HOLDING OUR LADDERS.

But if we want to climb a fifty-foot ladder, we'll need the very best people holding it. Even those who were able to hold the medium-height ladder aren't capable unless, of course, they've grown in their strength and skill. It goes without saying that those who hold our ladders don't have to understand everything we're doing when

25. Cited by Michelle Hespe, Editor-in-Chief of *The CEO Magazine*, "The Key to Culture," www.the-ceo-magazine.com.

we're climbing, but they at least need to know that we're going up instead of sideways! Our vision of growth has become their vision of growth, too.[26]

CORE COMPETENCIES

What are the characteristics we're looking for in those who hold our ladders? We need to see these qualities as they already exist, yet we also need to see potential for greater development. We can use the acronym "STAFF" to describe the core competencies:

STRONG

The people we select and train need to have strong characters, strong values, and strong hearts. They aren't fragile. They are able to receive instructions, give creative ideas, and handle criticism without flinching. (If they flinch, we fall!)

TEACHABLE

The ones holding our ladders need open minds. They realize narrow-minded certainty severely limits creativity and the ability to come up with new ideas. They're readers and they're self-motivated to learn more. When someone has a novel idea, they don't respond by reflexively discarding the concept. They say, "That's interesting, but I don't quite understand. Explain it to me in more detail."

ATTENTIVE

When people are holding my ladder, I don't want them to be distracted! They need to notice when the ladder is shaking (and it will from time to time), when I need help, and when I need an additional tool so I can perform my role more effectively. These people listen and internalize instructions, so you don't have to tell them the same things over and over again. When we tell them something, they get it.

FIRM

The people at the bottom of our ladders need to have solid footing so they aren't pushed off balance by people who use criticism or praise to

26. The principles and practices described in this section come from my book, *Who's Holding Your Ladder* (New Kensington, PA: Whitaker House, 2016).

manipulate them. They recognize sarcastic and subtle ways people try to inject doubt about the leader's capability or purposes. They see yellow flags (and maybe red ones) when others approach them with questions and comments such as, "Have you noticed this about our boss?" "Do you know anything about what's really going on?" "Did you hear that? That can't be right!" These conversations don't happen in staff meetings. They occur in hallways, restrooms, parking lots, and, increasingly today, on social media.

FAITHFUL

Those who are holding our ladders need to have faith in us as their leaders. If they doubt our integrity or competence, they won't be dedicated to helping us climb as high as possible and they won't devote themselves to becoming stronger and more skilled at holding our ladders. Without this confidence in us, we can only use a footstool. From the first day we hire someone, that person needs to have at least a modicum of faith in us. Over time, the relationship develops, trust matures, and faith grows. We are foolish, though, to retain people whose hands are on our ladders if they don't genuinely believe in us.

JESUS'S EXAMPLE OF LEADERSHIP

Jesus was a leader who developed His people. He followed a simple and effective four-step model:

1. I do it and you watch me.
2. Let's do it together.
3. You do it and I'll watch you.
4. You're on your own.

For the first part of His ministry, Jesus let the disciples watch Him as He healed the sick, calmed the seas, cast out demons, and cared for the poor. Increasingly, He involved them in His work. For instance, He told them to take the bread and fish He had broken and pass it out to feed more than five thousand hungry people on the hillside. (See Matthew 14:13–21; Mark 6:31–44; Luke 9:12–17; John 6:1–14.) Twice in the Gospels, we see Jesus send people out to spread His ministry: the twelve apostles one time (see Matthew 10:1–42; Luke 9:1–6) and seventy-two disciples another time (see Luke 10:1–17). In the end, they were on their own.

Because of the fruits of their labors, Christianity today has more than two billion followers, making it the most widely practiced religion in the world, transforming individuals and cultures with the message of Jesus's love, kindness, integrity, and power. If we follow this example, we may not raise the dead or perform miracles, but we *can* gradually equip and empower people to do more than they ever dreamed possible.

Selecting the best people to hold our ladders is only the first step. We then need to develop them. We need to train our people in how to accomplish tasks, but even more, we need to develop them in their leadership, teamwork, and communication skills. For instance, a pastor may train a greeter to smile, open the door, and welcome people to the service, but he also wants to develop the greeter to have an eye to notice those who need additional care and a heart to reach out with compassion. As she stands at the door smiling and greeting people, she is always looking for those who appear hesitant, have babies in their arms, are new to the church, or are drenched from a sudden downpour. The greeter notices and takes action to care for those people. Of course, the pastor wants people who can do the nuts and bolts of getting jobs accomplished, but he also takes the time to instill the "softer side of leadership" in those who serve in every capacity in the church.

The same qualities are important in businesses and nonprofits. Leaders develop those around them to look beyond their tasks, their definable objectives, to care for people in ways that are sometimes far beyond their job descriptions.

Development is the human connection in any organization. It includes a range of commitments that are modeled and encouraged, such as the ability to disagree agreeably, respecting people even when we disagree with them, and asking second and third questions instead of jumping to conclusions and immediately defending our position.

Most of the companies and organizations where I consult are long on training but short on development; people know what's expected of them, but the leaders often haven't taken the time to really get to know their people, to find out their highest hopes and uncover their deepest fears. They may have very detailed job descriptions and elaborate reporting structures, but relationships are sometimes a train wreck and unresolved conflict is a poisonous cloud in every room. Training is essential, but it's not complete without developing strong, enduring relationships. When we connect with people at a deeper human

TRAINING IS EASY; DEVELOPMENT TAKES MORE EFFORT, HEART, AND SKILL, BUT IT MAKES ALL THE DIFFERENCE IN CREATING A GREAT TEAM.

level, vulnerability can create strong bonds of trust; we model empathy, which is the glue of meaningful relationships. The people holding our ladders need both training and development. Training is easy; development takes much more effort, heart, and skill, but it makes all the difference in creating a great team.

EMPOWERING A TEAM

Leaders empower people on their teams by injecting meaning into everything they do. Empowerment is much more than delegation of responsibility. It is that, of course, but we rev people's engines when they're convinced that what they do each day has an impact on the lives of others. They're not just making widgets; they're making widgets to improve the quality of life for the people who use them. We motivate those on our teams when we ask them to speak into an important decision and we listen to their input. When they believe they have a voice, they're more engaged, more committed, and more energized, even when the decision wasn't what they suggested.

In some organizations, people are always looking over their shoulders to see if they're going to be slapped down for doing something wrong or having a novel idea. But in a healthy culture, they have a zone of safety and they feel secure. This security doesn't foster lethargy; it's the fertile soil of creativity and innovation. (If someone takes advantage of this positive environment by slacking off, you'll know that person either needs to connect tasks with purpose more fully, or he needs to go.)

When leaders empower others, they are giving power away. The people on the team have the opportunity—in fact, the authority—to take more initiative to come up with better ideas and methods, which almost inevitably leads to greater motivation to achieve higher results. The very best leaders don't insist on being the center of attention and having all the right ideas. They push authority and responsibility to lower levels in the organization, bringing out the best in their people and celebrating like crazy when each one succeeds. After a successful event, the leader may tell the team, "That was amazing! We can tweak a few things, but let's talk about all the things that went really well so we can leverage those even more next time."

When things don't work out like they hoped, gifted leaders don't berate the people whose project came up short. These leaders dissect what went right even more than what went wrong. And they express confidence that the person leading that effort will have a better outcome next time.

In this environment and in these conversations, people on the team feel respected, honored, valued, admired, and confident in the leader. They are highly motivated to dive into the next project and give it their very best. They develop a wonderful blend of pride in their accomplishments and humility that it took the whole team pulling together to pull it off.

People live for affirmation, and they shrivel and wilt without it. Give it, but give it authentically. Don't just say the same bland niceties again and again. Become skilled at being specific in your encouragement. Notice particular qualities. Specific, thoughtful affirmations are much more powerful than "You're the best!" or "Great job!"

The best leaders are masters at catching people doing something innovative and affirming them for it and these leaders are skilled at using mistakes and failures as stepping stones of growth. They actually encourage people to keep trying and stretching because the only people who don't make mistakes are either dead or cowards. Most people are ashamed when they make mistakes, but in a healthy culture, people are free to admit their errors. If it was a good attempt but failed, the leader can help them learn and move on. If the failure was the result of a dumb decision, the leader can patiently help the person think through the process so it doesn't happen again. And if it was a great idea but the wrong time, the leader will encourage the person to keep pushing and innovating. The best leaders don't delight in being the center of attention and being the only one with good ideas. Quite the opposite. They delight in seeing others succeed and their delight is obvious to everyone.

THE PEOPLE AROUND YOU

If we look carefully, we'll notice four types of people in our organizations. When we identify them, we can tailor our communication—and our expectations—to fit each person. These include:

WANDERERS

These are people who can hear our vision again and again, but it doesn't sink in. We can take them to conferences, give them books, send links to podcasts, and share our hearts with them, but they just don't get the picture. They're not evil or immoral, but for some reason, they can't see beyond their own needs and desires. They sit in a cubicle and perform their assigned tasks, but they can't connect what they do to a higher purpose. If they serve as volunteers, they don't go beyond the minimum expectations. They wander in and out of our doors without connecting with the heart of our mission. They're undoubtedly the *wrong* people to ask to lead in your company or organization, but they aren't *bad* people.

FOLLOWERS

Many people get excited about the vision, but they don't take initiative to fulfill it. They see a need, but they assume someone else will take care of it. However, when a leader asks them to participate to meet the need, they're glad to help. Most people in our churches and many in our companies fall into this category.

ACHIEVERS

We love these people. They catch fire when they hear the vision and they invest their hearts, talents, and resources to make it happen. When they see a need, they don't hesitate: they take care of it. They come up with new ideas and they're supportive of others on the team. They're excited about being developed so they can be more effective in changing lives, not just trained to do the job.

LEADERS

A few people in our organizations are captured by the vision, devote everything in them to achieve it, and enlist others to join them in the work. They know, they grow, and they show. If we expect everyone on our teams to be this kind of person, we may be deeply disappointed. At higher levels of an organization, though, such as the executive team, every person should be an exceptional leader. As the organization grows, we need to be more selective about the people we select, train, and develop. We look for more leaders to join us.

When I speak on this topic, I tell the audience, "Within a day or two after this event, you'll know which category you fit into. Some of you will leave here and call a friend to share what you've learned because this information may help him or her. You may be a leader. Some of you will go home and review your notes so you can internalize the concepts so you can grow. You're probably an achiever. If you don't bother to look at your notes, you may be a follower. And if you've missed the talks because you were walking around outside, you're a wanderer."

NOT AN OPTION

Great leaders know that they can only grow their organizations to the extent they're developing effective, passionate leaders. To them, leadership development isn't just one of the ancillary programs; it's central to the organization's life and health. In an article for Leadership Network, Brent Dolfo identifies some of the most important principles that leaders of churches, and by extension, every organization, need to implement, including:

- "Each church embodies a vision so large that it cannot be accomplished with the current paid staff and volunteer leaders." The vision drives the need for more manpower to fulfill it.

- "Someone on the senior team wakes up each day thinking about leadership development." It doesn't just happen; someone must own the strategy and drive the implementation.

+ "Each church has embraced the idea that building leaders and multiplying them for God's kingdom is their kingdom work." There are no dead ends on the organizational chart. Every person in leadership is tasked with recruiting, placing, and training more leaders.

+ "Each church focuses on building leaders from within." They don't rely on hiring stars from outside the organization. They recruit and place carefully and they make coaching an integral part of developing all their people.

+ "Great churches have metrics on their dashboards that tell them if they're winning in developing leaders." They don't make assumptions that leadership development will happen automatically. They ask, "What percent of our staff were developed internally, and which were from the outside? What percent of our leaders are actively, intentionally coaching their people? How many people are in each phase of the leadership pipeline?"[27]

Some CEOs and company presidents feel they're too busy to invest time in coaching their people, or maybe they've never seen it themselves, so they don't know how to develop people. Whatever the reason, it's not an excuse to neglect this central aspect of leadership. Developing those under us is an investment that pays the biggest dividends in sharpened skills, passion, and trust.

TRUST IS NEVER STATIC: IT IS EITHER BEING BUILT, SHATTERED, OR SLOWLY ERODED.

THE ESSENTIALS FOR TRUST ON A TEAM

Teams rise or fall on their level of trust. When suspicion permeates thoughts, people feel forced to protect themselves, dominate others, or demand respect. Trust is much more important than organizational

27. "10 Truths of Churches that Do a Great Job with Leadership Development," Brent Dolfo, Leadership Network, January 15, 2016, https://leadnet.org/ten-truths-of-churches-that-do-a-great-job-with-leadership-development-part-1.

structures, reporting systems, titles, and accolades. Trust is never static: it is either being built, shattered, or slowly eroded. The essential components of trust on a team include:

PROFICIENCY

We need people who can do the job assigned to them. They may be growing in their talents, but they need to at least have minimum capabilities so we don't have to look over their shoulders all the time. The rest of the people on the team also need to know that each person is capable. Proficiency can always be honed, refined, and expanded. Today, leadership isn't about being the best in every area; it's being a coordinator of specialists.

INTEGRITY

Trust is built when people are honest at their own expense, it's eroded when others suspect the person isn't telling the truth, and it's shattered when lies are uncovered. Another part of integrity is being the same person in a meeting as in private conversations. Gossip and slander may contain an element of truth, but they are sinister power plays to harm another person's reputation.

VULNERABILITY

When people trust each other, they can take steps to be more open about their dreams and fears. We don't expect people to share everything, but a team that is growing in trust gradually shares more about their hearts, not just their performance. Quite often, tragedies are the catalyst for breaking down walls between people. In those times, we see who moves in to heal the hurt and who backs away.

DEDICATION

The leaders of healthy teams welcome new ideas and aren't shocked by disagreements. People who trust each other feel free to offer competing ideas, but they have a shared commitment to their common vision (what they want to achieve), their common mission (how they'll achieve it), and their common core values (the non-negotiable philosophy and practices of the organization).

EMPATHY

The very best relationships are characterized by empathy, the ability to walk around in another person's skin, to feel what he feels and see what he sees. In some ways, the highest goal of a leader is for the people on the team to feel understood. It's not enough for the leader to sit back and analyze team members and give instructions. The people on the team need to know the leader "gets them." When they do, amazing things will happen.

As we create an environment where trust can grow stronger, we'll realize some people thrive, but others resist. In a dynamic organization, leaders have three responsibilities in relating to their teams: to sift, shift, and lift. After we've given people plenty of opportunities to invest in the good of the team, we may discover some simply don't fit, so we *sift* the team to know who stays and who goes. We may also realize some people are better suited for a different role than the one currently assigned, so we *shift* them laterally to a different role. And we discover a few people have exemplary character and talents, so we *lift* them to a higher responsibility.

Many teams and their leaders experience a high degree of awkwardness when it's time for someone to leave. Of course, some partings are short and sharp because of a breach of trust, but far more often, we can create a smoother path for people to move on. It's unreasonable to expect total loyalty to our businesses or us as leaders.

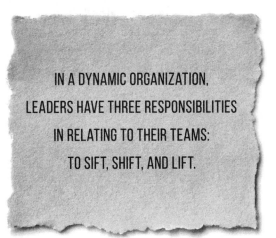

IN A DYNAMIC ORGANIZATION, LEADERS HAVE THREE RESPONSIBILITIES IN RELATING TO THEIR TEAMS: TO SIFT, SHIFT, AND LIFT.

We live in a mobile society and people change jobs for a myriad of reasons. Our job is to avoid taking it personally when someone decides to leave. Then we can make transitions as painless as possible for all involved.

I've known a few leaders who were experts at opening channels of communication before their staff members even thought about a move. From time to time, they announced in staff meetings, "I really appreciate your commitment to your role, but let's be honest: people sometimes change jobs. If and when you feel the urge to move, talk to me about it. We may be able to find another role that fits you better here, or you may want to go somewhere else. No matter what happens, I want the transition to be smooth. And I want us to remain friends. Can we do that?"

I've realized I'm only as effective as the people on my team. I've learned to find the right people, give them plenty of rope, encourage them to do their very best, and celebrate their successes. I used to be much more anxious about what would get done, but with my new thinking, I can now hold things more loosely.

However, there are a few things leaders must always hold in their hands. Leaders can't delegate vision; they must own it. They can't delegate culture; they must craft it. They can't delegate relationships with the primary stakeholders; they must cultivate them. They can't delegate the development of their teams; they must devote themselves to it. If we become this kind of leader, the very best people will stand in line to join our teams.

Don't be like Larry Brown, coaching a collection of superstars who can't play together. Be like coxswain Bobby Moch on the University of Washington rowing team, steering and giving direction to the passionate, dedicated, skilled, and specialized people in front of you.

THINK ABOUT IT...

1. Look at the "Lessons from a Rowing Team." Which of these is a strength of your leadership? Which needs some improvement?

2. Identify the health of your organizational culture: inspiring, accepting, stagnant, discouraging, or toxic. Explain your answer.

3. What are some signs of mutual respect on a team? Where have you experienced this? What difference did it make for you?

4. Are your direct reports holding your ladder with strength, integrity, and skill so you can climb as high as you want to climb? Why or why not?

5. What are some differences between delegating tasks and empowering people?

6. What are you doing to build and maintain trust on your team? What do you need to do better? What difference will it make?

8

HOW DO I HANDLE CONFLICT?
THE QUESTION OF EXPECTATIONS

When I get ready to talk to people,
I spend two thirds of the time thinking what they want to hear
and one third thinking about what I want to say.
—Abraham Lincoln

I heard about a man who was shipwrecked on a desert island far out in the Pacific. There were no living animals on the island—no lizards, no crickets, no birds. He was completely alone. Years later, a ship finally passed by and saw his distress signal. When they pulled close, the man yelled that he was glad to be rescued. The captain of the ship looked at the little island and asked him, "Before we bring you on board, would you mind giving me a tour of the island?"

The man protested, "What? I've been here alone for years. I'm the only person here on the island. I want to leave as soon as I can." But he agreed to give the captain a tour.

The two men walked down the beach to a hut. The captain asked, "What's this?"

The man explained, "I made this out of palm branches to get me out of the sun and rain. It's my home."

A little farther down the beach, they came to another shelter. The captain asked, "Why do you need two houses?"

The man shook his head, "This isn't a house. It's my church. I wanted to be able to go somewhere besides my hut to church, so I built this. I leave home to go to church here."

The men walked down the beach a little more and they came to a third shelter. The captain looked perplexed. He asked, "What's this for?"

The man told him, "That's the church I used to go to."

Jesus told His followers, "*Where two or three gather in my name, there am I with them*" (Matthew 18:20). But from my observations, that sometimes doesn't seem to be true. I've been in churches where thousands gathered in the name of Jesus, but you could cut the tension in the air with a knife. It sure didn't seem like Jesus was there with them!

SOMETHING TO PROVE

I know something about conflict. It's not just academic to me. When I was in the third and fourth grades, I got into fights every day. Most of the boys were bigger than me and they beat me up every time we fought. Each time, they thought the fight was over and they assumed I'd never get into another scuffle with them, but that's not what happened. Every afternoon after school, I jumped out from behind a wall or a tree, gave them a couple of shots with my fists, and tried to run away before they grabbed me and started pounding the life out of me.

I remember those boys looking at me after they pummeled me for the hundredth time. They had been sure nobody in their right mind would want to fight if he lost every time, but I kept coming. They started to avoid me. Maybe they thought I was crazy, or maybe they were afraid they might do permanent damage and they didn't want that on their consciences. No, kids don't think like that. They probably saw me more as a nuisance than a threat. I never won a fight in my life, but I was tenacious, like a rabid little Chihuahua—I never quit. Just because the fight was over for them didn't mean it was over for me. I always had something to prove.

Years later, this experience gave me insights about the powerful and often hidden motives of people engaged in conflict.

EXPECTATIONS AND REALITY

Dr. Tim Elmore, the president of Growing Leaders, observes that conflict is "natural, normal, and neutral" in all meaningful relationships.[28] In fact, it's unavoidable.

+ It's *natural* because we're fallen people and we live in a fallen world.

+ It's *normal* because people have different perspectives and agendas.

+ It's *neutral* because we can use it to be either constructive or destructive; it's our choice.

Many people get freaked out by conflict because they don't have confidence in how to deal with it. But disagreement and dissension are part of life. In the natural world, we see conflict among plant species for soil, water, and light, and we see conflict among animals for food, dominance, and mating rights. Virtually every great story, ancient or modern, revolves around people in conflict. We could easily say the entire Bible is about people in conflict with God and each other—and how God steps in to provide wisdom, forgiveness, and healing, but only for those who are willing to take His hand and enter the process. We experience disputes with our spouses, parents, children, neighbors, and friends, in the workplace and in every other conceivable area of life. Even when people die, they often leave a lot of unfinished business with their families. If you insist on creating a world without conflict, you'll have to say nothing, do nothing, and be nothing.

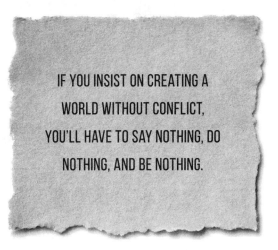

IF YOU INSIST ON CREATING A WORLD WITHOUT CONFLICT, YOU'LL HAVE TO SAY NOTHING, DO NOTHING, AND BE NOTHING.

---

28. Cited in "Emancipating from Marriage Myths," *The Star* (Jamaica), August 2, 2016, https://www.pressreader.com/jamaica/the-star-jamaica/20160802/281552290234699.

Some people create conflict so they can push people off-balance and control them; on the other end of the spectrum, others see all conflict as inherently sinful, or at least the product of sin. They feel so uncomfortable with any tension that they go to the extreme of labeling the feeling, event, or person as "evil." Their conclusion is that good and godly leaders never allow even a hint of conflict. Their beliefs, expectations, and fears cause them to want instant answers and immediate solutions. They don't have the wisdom to welcome tension as a tool for growth.

Conflict is caused by the distance between expectations and reality. When the distance is significant, people clash. Here's an illustration: a husband walks out the door and his wife asks, "What time will you be home?" His answer creates an expectation. If he gives her a time that's unreasonable, either too early or too late, he's foolish! He could say, "Honey, you may be out of my presence, but you're always on my mind." If he gives her a time, like 7 o'clock, he has created a specific expectation. If he shows up at 7:30, the reality is a significant distance from her expectation and she's upset. If he comes through the door at 9:00, the distance is even farther and she's hopping mad! If he looks at his watch on the way home and it's after 10:00, he should probably sleep in the car that night. In all cases, the distance between expectation and reality determines the level of conflict.

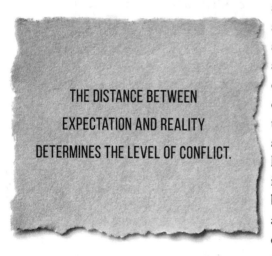

THE DISTANCE BETWEEN EXPECTATION AND REALITY DETERMINES THE LEVEL OF CONFLICT.

Let's turn the tables around. Some men (like me) are pretty dense. We take things at face value, which can be both foolish and dangerous. Let me give an example: a husband walks in the house and he can tell something is wrong. He asks his wife a simple, direct question, "What's wrong?" When she gives that one-word answer, "Nothing," he thinks, *Okay, great. I'll turn on the TV and watch the game.* Her expectation was for her husband to read her mood, be engaged, pursue her, delve deep into her emotional state, and invite her to share her deepest feelings. Wrong! Her expectation was met with the reality of his lack of understanding. This time, though, conflict may be subterranean for hours or days before she finally tells him she's hurt that he's so insensitive. During all that time, he's totally clueless.

When a wide gap between expectations and reality continues, conflict has many negative consequences:

+ It pushes us away from sound judgments because we're afraid to be honest.

+ It causes us to have hidden agendas in every meeting and conversation.

+ It creates the need to control people so they don't hurt us again.

+ It isolates us and makes us defensive.

+ It shatters or erodes trust.

+ It consumes our thoughts, distracts us, and saps our energy so we accomplish far less.

+ It makes leading so hard that we may want to quit.

But this doesn't have to be the narrative of our lives and our leadership! If we close the gap between expectations and reality, some wonderful things happen:

+ We gain enormous wisdom because we wrestle with the things that really matter to us and to others.

+ We build trust as people realize we care about them and are willing to wade into disagreements without fear or demands.

+ We make better decisions because our minds aren't clouded by empty hopes and misguided fears.

+ The people on our teams are more committed to decisions because they feel heard and understood.

Instead of being afraid of conflict or using it to manipulate people, great leaders realize conflict is expected and, to a certain extent, desirable when people are passionately engaged in the goals of the organization. If we're not eliciting their best ideas and deepest emotions, we aren't getting the most out of them. As growth accelerates and people see how their ideas are bearing fruit, they become even more involved and enthusiastic and conflict may increase. Though we're not surprised by rising tensions as the organization moves forward, we don't sit back and let conflict have poisonous effects. We engage, use diplomacy, and teach our people the principles of listening, communicating, and negotiating.

THE RED FLAG SIGNAL

I've noticed that the red flag signal of conflict almost always includes two simple words: "I thought." These words look innocent enough on paper, but they speak volumes about the person's perception of the distance between expectation and reality.

+ He tells the police officer, "I thought I was doing 35 miles an hour."

+ She tells her husband, "I thought you said you'd be home by 7 o'clock."

+ A staff member says, "I thought the report was due tomorrow."

+ A friend grumbles, "I thought you were going to pay for dinner."

+ An employee tells a boss, "I thought I was getting a raise."

+ A boss tells a manager, "I thought your numbers would be better than this."

We can come up with an endless number of examples because the field of our expectations is unbounded. We need to learn to ask the right question. When we find ourselves in conflict, the first question we ask should not be, "How can I fight back so I can win?" or "How can I get out of this as quickly as possible?" Those are fight or flight responses and they do nothing to help us think more accurately about what's going on in front of us. A far better question is, "What was the expectation?" If we can identify and articulate the expectation, we'll go a long way toward bridging the gap between it and reality.

Why do we focus on expectations instead of reality? Because people often become defensive and defiant about their views of reality and they seldom budge. They are usually much more willing to talk about what they hoped or expected to happen.

The expectation is the *what* of the conflict. It helps us be objective and calm so we can have a productive discussion. When people jump to the *who* and use "you" statements, the other person immediately feels attacked and becomes defensive. Then, the conflict shifts from the original issue to the immediate issue of the unfair attack—and that's inevitably how it's perceived.

Instead of saying, "You left the door unlocked," we can say, "The door was left unlocked." Instead of the accusatory, "Don't you know how to run the sound system?" we can say, "The sound wasn't very clear today. What can we do to fix it so it doesn't happen again?" We keep the same message but remove the blame. Using the word "you" throws a match into a vat of gasoline—you don't have to wait long for the explosion! At some point in the discussion, there will be time to assign appropriate responsibility for what happened, but avoid that moment as long as possible. When the *what* has been sufficiently discussed, the person knows you aren't out for blood (which is how "you" statements are interpreted) and the emotions are quiet, so it's easier for us to say, "What are you going to do differently next time?" Even in this statement, we're pointing forward and offering hope for improvement.

THE EXPECTATION IS THE *WHAT* OF THE CONFLICT. IT HELPS US BE OBJECTIVE AND CALM SO WE CAN HAVE A PRODUCTIVE DISCUSSION.

Watch out for extreme terms like "always" and "never." Hyperbole may be useful in poetry and novels, but not in dialogue with people we love and serve. When we're frustrated with someone or we don't feel understood, we may inflate our words to make our points stronger. Yes, they sound stronger, but it's counter-productive. These words make the speaker feel powerful and they shut the other person down, intimidate, and close off meaningful conversation. Solomon gave us a revolutionary principle: "*A gentle tongue can break a bone*" (Proverbs 25:15). This means a soft answer can break down a person's defenses so he can hear us. It's important to "power down," relax, and try to communicate in a way that builds the relationship instead of damaging it. You can say, "I think I see a pattern here. Let's talk about it so we can resolve it and move forward."

+ Focus on the *what*.

+ Avoid "you" until after discussing the *what*.

+ Avoid terms like "always" and "never."

+ Point to a hopeful future by asking, "What are you going to do next time?"

When we blow up at someone, we may be right that the person has been less than responsible, but we've taken big steps backward in the relationship, we've contaminated the water of trust and respect that is necessary for healthy connections, and we can't un-ring that bell. It'll take a lot more time, apologies, and patience to rebuild the relationship.

RESOLUTION...OR NOT

Many people think they're resolving conflict when they try to lower the tension level so people aren't as angry or hurt any longer. That's only managing emotions, not resolving the source of the conflict. People who want to be seen as nice have great difficulty going below the surface and having real conversations about the *what* of the conflict. They'd rather say, "Oh, it didn't bother me," or "She couldn't help it," or "I don't know what you're talking about. There's no conflict!" In stark contrast, others see every moment of tension as a cosmic battle for dominance. They feel threatened and their way of handling it is to win at all costs. They use blame and name-calling, they get loud, and they glare menacingly at the other person. Still others take a third approach: they give in, absorb all the blame, and do their best to get the tension over immediately. We often find all these responses on the same team and in the same family.

Far too often, people make two mistakes: they want everyone to feel better right away and they invest their energies in resolving the momentary event instead of addressing patterns and underlying issues. The event happened because someone felt misunderstood, someone had unrealistic expectations, or someone didn't communicate expectations and left the other person guessing (and usually guessing wrong). The expectations need to be brought to the surface, analyzed, and addressed. The event is merely the field where the expectations played out their game. It would be silly for people watching a football game, baseball game, or soccer match to look constantly at the field. They keep their eyes on the players. That's where the action is!

When relationships are tense, people naturally want to assign blame... to someone else. In most conflicts, both parties bear some responsibility, at least for not communicating clearly enough in the early stage of the difficulty. Of course, in some cases of abuse, the blame is all on one side, but that's rare. Instead of doing mental and emotional gymnastics to be sure to deflect blame to the other person, wise people—those who have learned to think clearly in times of tension—look to the future more than the past. They are able to accept responsibility for their part in what happened and just as importantly, they assume responsibility for what happens next. They're willing to ask good questions and listen, really listen, to the heart of the other person. Quite often, hurt and anger subside substantially when people feel heard and understood. That's the first and most important goal: to understand the other person's expectations and for them to know you understand.

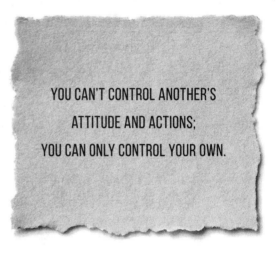

YOU CAN'T CONTROL ANOTHER'S ATTITUDE AND ACTIONS; YOU CAN ONLY CONTROL YOUR OWN.

If the other person doesn't care a rip about your expectations, don't get into a verbal (or physical) fight. That person may need time to decompress, trust that you really do care enough to want to understand, and then begin to listen to you. You can't control another's attitude and actions; you can only control your own.

In many cases, our responses to stress—and stress-inducing people— are hardwired in us from years of responding in the same ways. We don't even think about how to respond; we just react. The people around us see our misplaced expectations, but if we're not aware of them, we'll use them to bludgeon the people we love and serve.

A few years ago, a well-known pastor invited me to speak at a leadership roundtable at his church. Before the first session began, we had a very warm and cordial conversation in his office. We left to go to the meeting room and as we walked through the door into the room where tables were set up, his countenance radically changed. At first, he didn't say a word, but his face got red, his jaw tightened, and his fists clenched. He was furious! I asked, "Are you okay? Is there something I need to know or do?"

Without turning to me, he snapped, "When will they get it? What's wrong with those people?"

I wasn't sure I should follow up with a question or grab a glass of water to toss on him to cool him down, but I asked, "What's the matter? It looks fine to me."

"I told them to set up tables and chairs."

I looked around. "Uh, that's what they've done."

He barked, "I wanted *round* tables, not these *rectangles*! I wanted the chairs set on one side of the round tables facing the front. They should have known that!"

Ahh. Now I knew. I said, "So, you didn't exactly *tell* them you wanted *round* tables?"

"No," he growled. "I told you—they should have known." After a few seconds of indignation, he turned to me and asked, "What do I need to do, Sam? Draw pictures for them?"

I smiled. "Yes! If you'd taken ten seconds to draw a picture on a napkin for them, they would have understood exactly what you wanted."

He bristled at my observation and I could tell he was trying to find a way to deflect my suggestion. I didn't back away. I said gently, "My friend, own it. You could have communicated very easily and very well, but you didn't. They did exactly what they thought you expected them to do. Don't blame them for that. That's on you."

The people who communicate set the expectation and then they need to own it. No dodging or hiding, no blame-shifting, no bluster to intimidate. They need to take responsibility for the implied promise that's inherent in every expectation.

Some leaders, like this pastor, don't communicate expectations at all. They insist, "Why should I have to tell her (or him or them) again? She should know what I expect." Implied expectations often lead to conflict because what's implied by one person can easily be missed by another, leaving a yawning gap between expectations and reality. Certainly, if a couple has lived together for decades, they will probably have a good idea what their spouse likes and expects, but my hunch is that the majority of conflicts in marriages happen because at least one person didn't make one expectation clear…and then another and another, until a backlog of small infractions builds into a big problem.

As leaders, we sometimes think we've communicated clearly, but we leave people guessing. I may announce to my team, "Our meeting tomorrow morning is at 9 o'clock. I'd like you to be there early." But what does "early" mean? From my request, they don't know what I expect. Do I want them there at 8:30, at 8:45, or at 8:59? All of these times qualify as "early." If I expected them to show up at 8:00, I'd start getting really ticked off at 8:15. By the time the first person shows up at 8:30, I'll be fuming and snarl, "Where have you been?"

When the meeting does begin and everyone was actually "early," they have no idea why I'm boiling. During the entire staff meeting, all of us are preoccupied with my completely disproportionate emotions rather than being able to focus on the agenda.

You might read this scenario and claim, "I don't do that." Oh, really? Do you ever ask anyone to get back to you "ASAP"? Do you write that as the deadline on a memo of instructions? If you've ever used that term, you've created a confused expectation. Some who are driven and want to please will make sure they get the job done really soon and you'll be happy. However, those who take it as a genuine mandate to get the job done "as soon as possible" when it works out in their flow of responsibilities may get back to you much later than you expected. At that point, you're frustrated at the person's "irresponsible behavior," but, in fact, you're the one who stated an unclear expectation, which created confusion and conflict.

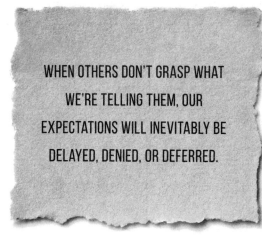

WHEN OTHERS DON'T GRASP WHAT WE'RE TELLING THEM, OUR EXPECTATIONS WILL INEVITABLY BE DELAYED, DENIED, OR DEFERRED.

When I talk to clients, I try to be crystal clear. When I give them an assignment, I ask them when they can get back to me. If they say, "Sometime next week," I don't know when it's coming. If they say, "Next Wednesday," that's better. If they tell me, "I'll send it to you by noon next Wednesday," my client's responsibility is as clear as my expectation. When I'm working with most people, my "as soon as possible" is always sooner than their possible. Being clear solves a multitude of problems.

Most people have some degree of "mental slippage." In a meeting or across the dinner table, we say something that's clear to us, but it doesn't stick in the other person's mind: it slips out. Because the person nodded or moaned, we assume she's got it. She may or she may not. (This is especially common in children and it's chronic in teenagers. If a point is important, it's much better to repeat it a few times or ask the person to repeat it back to us so we know it's stuck. When others don't grasp what we're telling them, our expectations will inevitably be delayed, denied, or deferred.

RESPONDING TO DIFFICULT PEOPLE

We could make a long list of the types of people who give leaders problems. I only want to highlight a representative sample. Leaders need to be able to identify the traits of those who are:

+ Defiant (they're pretty easy to spot)

+ Too compliant (do we see them as problems at all?)

+ Sneaky or passive-aggressive (they always have a hidden agenda)

+ Perfectionists (who never see good in anything)

+ Control freaks (who insist on determining every outcome)

In a leader's relationships with any of these people, there are two challenges: them and us. Yes, us. In a *Forbes* magazine article, Elizabeth B. Brown asks questions that help leaders understand why certain people pull our chains:

+ What emotional tornadoes does the difficult person in your life spin off?

+ How do you react to a difficult person in your life?

+ How does your difficult person react to your reactions?

+ If the other person is the problem, are you growing unhealthy actions and reactions in response to him or her?

+ Are you the difficult person driving others to reactive behavior?

+ How do others react to your actions and responses?

Brown writes:

Feeding into our frustrations when dealing with a difficult person can become a vicious cycle. We tend to see or hear an interaction and then interpret that action based, not on fact, but on our assumptions. Then we react. Unfortunately, we usually don't have all of the information as to why an individual may be showing up the way they are and, in the absence of factual information, we tend to fill in the blanks with our own theories about what might be going on.[29]

When we're aware of our triggers, we have more choices in how we respond. We can stay calm when faced with the anger and demands of defiant people. We ask good questions and make clear statements. We realize that outward compliance from some of our staff and family members doesn't necessarily mean hearty agreement. They may just be avoiding any hint of conflict because they're wounded and scared. We learn to confront passive-aggressive people to hold them accountable for smiling while they stab us in the back. Over time, we grow in wisdom to look beneath the surface to see the fears that drive people's responses and behavior.

---

29. "A Guide to Dealing with Difficult People," Chris Cancialosi, *Forbes*, March 5, 2018, https://www.forbes.com/sites/chriscancialosi/2018/03/05/a-guide-to-dealing-with-difficult-people/#3b32265a2293.

REFRAMING THE CONFLICT

If we can reframe the conflict, we won't take it as personally and we'll be able to address concrete problems instead of attacking the people involved. A simple and memorable acronym to help us stay on track is PLUS:

> OVER TIME, WE GROW IN WISDOM TO LOOK BENEATH THE SURFACE TO SEE THE FEARS THAT DRIVE PEOPLE'S RESPONSES AND BEHAVIOR.

PAUSE

Don't discount the person who has raised the conflict or contributed to it and don't rush to find the quickest solution because tension feels so uncomfortable. Stop to ask yourself some questions about your own response and define the *what*—the expectation—as clearly as possible.

LISTEN

Don't jump in to fix the person or the problem. Ask simple and direct questions, such as, "How do you see this situation?" and "What do you think we need to do about it?" When the person voices an opinion or a plan, issue an invitation: "Tell me more about that."

UNDERSTANDING

Remember that it's important for the person to feel understood, so after listening for a while, you might say, "Here's what I hear you saying," recap what they've told you, and then ask, "Is that right?" Sometimes, the person will say, "No, you missed it." If that's the case, try again.

SOLVE

Own your part of the tension and talk about how the two of you can solve the problem together. If you need to apologize, do it. If you need to forgive, do that. At least one of you—maybe both—will need to adjust expectations in the future. If the relationship is irreparably harmed, be honest about that reality. As much as possible, have a gracious parting.

DON'T LET IT GET TOO PERSONAL

Wise leaders create environments where disagreement is constructive and accepted by everyone at the table. But these leaders also have finely-tuned antennae to realize when disagreements become too personal, which creates defensiveness and soon devolves into bitter conflict. Leaders who create a culture of openness and creativity welcome disagreements because they signal their people are giving their best, but these leaders step in to nip corrosive conflict in the bud before it causes significant and even irreparable damage.

To become this kind of leader, you have to be secure enough to be comfortable with people who disagree with you.

THINK ABOUT IT...

1. What are some examples in your life—maybe from the past week—when conflict was caused by a gap between expectations and reality?

2. What are the negative consequences of conflict you've seen (and endured) when it wasn't handled well? What are some benefits you've seen when you or another leader addressed tension with wisdom and grace?

3. What difference does it make to focus first on the *what* instead of the *who*?

4. Do those on your team (and people in your family) think you're crystal clear when you give instructions and set expectations? How do you know?

5. Take some time to reflect on the questions listed in the *Forbes* article. After you answer these, explain how understanding yourself better will help you be a more effective leader in times of disagreement and conflict.

6. How will using the PLUS strategy help you build relationships even during tense times with people?

9

HOW DO I COMMUNICATE MY VISION?
THE QUESTION OF CONNECTION

Five percent of the people think; ten percent of the people think
they think; and the other
eighty-five percent would rather die than think.
—Thomas A. Edison

When we look at how some leaders looked into the future, we get a good laugh:

+ In 1943, IBM President Thomas Watson said, "I think there is a world market for maybe five computers."

+ More recently and spectacularly wrong, Ken Olsen, founder of Digital Equipment Corporation, proclaimed confidently in 1977, "There is no reason anyone would want a computer in their home."

+ Darryl Zanuck, executive at Twentieth Century Fox, predicted in 1946, "Television won't be able to hold on to any market it captures after the first six months. People will soon get tired of staring at a plywood box every night."

+ When the Internet was in its fledgling phase, Robert Metcalfe, founder of 3Com, didn't believe it would last: "Almost all of the many predictions now being made about 1996 hinge on the Internet's continuing exponential growth. But I predict the Internet will soon go spectacularly supernova and in 1996 catastrophically collapse."

On the other hand, some leaders have been captured by a clear and compelling vision. To lure a top Pepsi executive to Apple, Steve Jobs asked, "Do you want to sell sugar water for the rest of your life, or do you want to come with me and change the world?" Elon Musk, founder of SpaceX and Tesla, Inc., didn't mince words when he gave SpaceX its marching orders: "We're going to land people on Mars by 2025." Some of us are old enough to remember the cartoon, *The Jetsons*. Everything in the family's life seemed absurd and unreachable only a few decades ago, but today we have FaceTime, cameras on drones, facial recognition software, instant meals, and driverless cars. The creators of *The Jetsons* may have thought they were only entertaining us, but they were describing a fantastic future that's becoming a reality today.

THE DISCONNECT

> LEADERS NEED TO COMMUNICATE IN THE *ABSTRACT* LANGUAGE OF VISION AND THE *CONCRETE* LANGUAGE OF EXECUTION.

Most CEOs, pastors, and other leaders I know don't have any trouble crafting their vision. They have a clear, powerful picture of where the company or organization needs to go and they have a comprehensive plan for the phases to get there. The problem is, they often have trouble translating their vision into the hearts and minds of their people. There is a disconnect: the way the leader thinks isn't the way the employees or team members think.

Leaders need to be bilingual. They have to communicate in the *abstract* language of vision and they have to speak in the *concrete* language of execution. The language of vision paints a picture of what will be and the benefits people will enjoy. It's long on motivation but short on strategies, roles, and processes. When leaders don't use this language effectively, the employees and staff become apathetic, ingrown, and competitive...and not in a good way. The language of execution explains the answer to our question: *Who does what by when?* People know what's expected of them, how to do it, where to find resources, and which benchmarks they need to reach along the way. When leaders fail to speak this language, people wander, they lose faith in their leader, and they go somewhere else so they can make a difference.

When they hear of any vision or change in plans, people instinctively want to know, *How does this affect me?* In a meeting of a corporate executive team, the CEO announces, "We're going to create a new line of products that will give us a presence in a new market." As he describes the big picture, the concrete mixer is already turning in the minds of those around the table.

The production manager is thinking, *What plant will we use? Who can I pull from our other jobs to work on this? When is the rollout? If he puts George in charge of the new product line, I'm quitting! I should get a promotion for all I do for the company!*

The CFO is thinking, *How much will this cost? What will be the cash flow challenges? How can we afford this?*

The marketing director wonders, *What's the hook for the new products? How do they fit in with our current promotions? What will my budget be? What are the sales quotas?*

And the CEO's administrative assistant thinks, *Oh, no! This is going to add so much to my workload! I was thinking about ways I could do less and now I'll have a lot more to do!*

The CEO was speaking the language of vision, but the people around the table were hearing the language of execution. He was in the clouds, but their minds were focused on the implications and implementation every second he was speaking. They fill in the missing concrete language with their own hopes and fears—and that's quick-setting concrete! It's necessary, then, for leaders to at least begin filling in the blanks at the earliest statement of the new vision. If not, they'll lose their people in blocks of concrete.

When leaders talk about the future, they need to continually speak in both languages. Many of the leaders I've known have told me, "Sam, I'm going to cast the vision the first week and give them the specifics the following week." I tell them that's a bad idea. That gives their people's concrete 168 hours to set up—and what sets up may not be close to the strategy, plans, and benchmarks the leader intended to tell them the next week. It's much harder to jackhammer their wrong, concrete assumptions the next week than to take the time to begin pouring the right concrete from the start.

Leaders need to communicate in both languages from the beginning and keep speaking both all along the way to completion. Both of these languages require the leader's energy, emotion, and time. Leaders need to prepare their staffs for the launch of a new project by speaking both abstractly and concretely so they get maximum buy-in. And they need to keep speaking in a bilingual way all along the process to maintain motivation and refine the assignments to each person.

In many companies, the word "reorganization" sends chills down people's spines. It flips a switch in their minds and they wonder:

Will I still have a job?

Will I be promoted?

Will I be demoted?

Will I get a raise?

Will I be given a nicer office?

Will I have to report to Sarah? I don't like her.

What will we stop doing? And what will we start doing?

Why do we have to go through this again? Haven't they learned anything?

Of course, the full picture of the vision may take longer than one meeting, so the leader needs to roll out part of the vision with the corresponding strategy, then the next part of the vision with the details that explain that plan, and so on until the entire vision is clear, strong, and understood by everyone. If they don't accurately grasp how the grand plan affects their lives, the leader hasn't been concrete enough.

Leaders need to avoid making the assumption that their people "should get it" when they talk about the future. When Satya Nadella took over as CEO of Microsoft, he soon realized he needed to change the culture by changing communication. When he arrived, the company's sense of vision and passion had eroded. He wanted to inject a new vitality into the culture by first letting his employees know that he understood them. In an interview for *Fast Company*, he explained:

> You have to be able to say, "Where is this person coming from? What makes them tick? Why are they excited or frustrated by something that is happening, whether it's about computing or beyond computing?"

Nadella realizes that he will only be a skilled leader if he continually learns his craft of innovating, leading, and communicating. He has been influenced by Stanford professor Carol Dweck's book, *Mindset*, "which outlines two types of thinking. Those who operate with a fixed mind-set are more likely to stick to activities that utilize skills they've already mastered, rather than risk embarrassment by failing at something new. Those

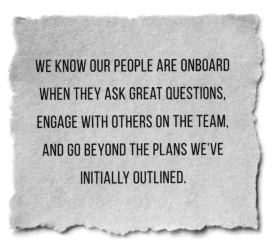

WE KNOW OUR PEOPLE ARE ONBOARD WHEN THEY ASK GREAT QUESTIONS, ENGAGE WITH OTHERS ON THE TEAM, AND GO BEYOND THE PLANS WE'VE INITIALLY OUTLINED.

focused on growth make it their mission to learn new things, understanding that they won't succeed at them all."[30] Some of us are natural visionaries; many are more gifted at defining processes and systems. But all of us can break out of our "fixed mind-set" to think, lead, and communicate more effectively.

What are some signs our communication of abstract ideas and concrete plans have connected with our people? We can be sure they're onboard when they come back to us with their own ideas, plans, marketing

30. "Leading While Learning," an interview with Satya Nadella, *Fast Company*, October 2017, FastCompany.com.

concepts, and connections to resources and other departments. They ask great questions, they engage with others on the team, and they go beyond the plans we've initially outlined. When they're excited and can't go to sleep because the vision keeps them up at night, you've connected with their deepest motivations.

If we've created a visionary culture, we sometimes only need to identify a need, paint a picture, and then stand back and see who steps up to meet it. A CEO might say, "It would be great if we could open another store on the west side of the city." The leader of a nonprofit might tell his staff, "I'd really like to see our unused office space refurbished for a childcare center." If they get no response, they need to invest more time and heart in creating a dynamic culture on the team. If they get a response, they may see people pour themselves into the task and show more creativity and determination than ever before.

SEVEN STEPS IN COMMUNICATING VISION

This, I admit, is a concrete way to describe the way leaders can roll out their vision so people will be inspired and motivated to support it.

1. CHASE THE DREAM

The vision of leaders is never static. It's always growing, sharpening, and developing. They're confident and happy, but they're never satisfied. There is a burning in their souls that reminds them there's always more to accomplish. Leaders continually feed themselves with input from great leaders, speakers, and coaches, and they can translate outstanding teaching from other fields into their own. They're not surprised when they think of a new idea that's beyond anything they've ever imagined. Their vision is dynamic and evolving, with different emphases in different seasons of their lives. In the first step, there's little form or substance to the dream—it's just an enticing idea that invites the leader to explore it.

2. CULTIVATE THE CONCEPT

Many leaders jump the gun and announce their new vision before it has had time to marinate and develop. They need time to cultivate it. They're wise to learn the lessons of farming: cultivate the soil, plant the seeds, nurture the plants, and then harvest the crop. The two that require the most time are cultivating the soil in the spring and nurturing the plants all summer. For leaders, "cultivate the concept" is analogous to a farmer cultivating the soil. It's a time of preparation, not planting, growth, or harvest...not yet anyway. During this time, there's a lot of work but little if anything for people to look at.

As the dream begins to take shape, the leader pulls out a pad and pen, or a smartphone and stylus, and begins cultivating the concept by conceptualizing a strategy. What will it look like when it's fulfilled? What stages will it take? What are the speedbumps? What resources will we need? In this stage, the leader crafts a comprehensive plan.

The planning process must coordinate activities with the normal calendar. For instance, it's unwise for a church to launch a growth strategy in the middle of summer; September and January are often the best times for initiatives to bring in new people. Business, too, revolves around predictable sales patterns. Many companies receive half of their revenues between Thanksgiving and Christmas, so executives spend much of the year getting ready for this brief but productive season. Mattresses often go on sale in March, while furniture sales are in July. In particular months, it's almost impossible to get a hotel room in some locations; at other times of the year, you can get the same rooms at a steep discount. All leaders need to match their planning and communication with the identifiable and predictable seasons.

3. CUT THE CROWD

I've learned to ask the question, "Who do I need to make this a reality?" Some people stand on the sidelines and cheer. That's great, but I need at least a few people in the arena with me who are willing to give their sweat, blood, toil, and tears to the effort. Some will make the cut; many won't. That doesn't make them bad people, but there are only a few who will be the closest aides.

4. CAST THE NET

When the vision and strategy are announced, look into the eyes of people to see who is instantly onboard with you. You're looking for early adopters, who can immediately add energy and enthusiasm to the cause.

But don't count the others out. Many of those who get on the wagon later are more reflective and sometimes more dedicated.

5. COMMIT TO CONSISTENCY

As the plan unfolds and is implemented, there will be plenty of challenges. We'll find out the cost is higher than we anticipated, some people we counted on don't come through, and we get behind schedule. Through all of this, we should not be surprised.

During the months and years of implementation, we continually align our resources—budget, personnel, time, facilities, programming, and energy—with the strategy and goals we've set out. No matter what, we don't give up. Vision plus alignment plus tenacity equals success.

6. CONNECT THE DOTS

Throughout the process, we're continually aware of the big picture of how the work toward the vision affects every part of the organization and we help our people see the connections, too. Nothing happens in a silo; everything happens in the open barn. This is one of the ways to manage expectations so people don't flip out when something that happens in another department has an impact on them and what they're doing.

7. CARE FOR THE PEOPLE

If we get to the goal but our people despise us for pushing them and blaming them, what have we really accomplished? In the end, our role as leaders is to improve the lives of the people around us; the fulfillment of the vision should have a positive impact on them. Care for them involves both empathy and action, intangibles and tangibles. I want to create meaning for each person so they can answer these questions:

- ♦ What defines me? (What gives me identity and purpose?)

- ♦ What are my deliverables? (What are the specific benefits of this work?)

- ♦ What are my delivery systems? (What is the process I'll use to impart the benefits to people?)

+ Who are my drivers? (Who are the people who make it happen?)

All change is a critique of the past. These questions help people navigate change so they can thrive in it. If they reflect on these issues, they'll probably find meaning in the middle of what otherwise might feel like a chaotic disruption of the status quo.

ALWAYS CONNECT THE DOTS

How often do we need to connect the dots for our people? Incessantly. A famous and terse statement Pastor Andy Stanley made years ago is universally true: "Vision leaks." He writes:

> Vision doesn't stick; it doesn't have natural adhesive. Instead, vision leaks. You've repeated the vision for your church a hundred times. Then someone will ask a question that makes you think, *What happened? Didn't they hear what we've said over and over? Don't they know what this church is all about?*

Instead of getting frustrated that people forget, drift, or lose focus on what we've said is the future of our organization, go back to the basics. Stanley asks himself piercing questions and comes to an important conclusion:

> What do I need to do to assure that we have a compelling vision as an organization, and what must I do to make sure it doesn't leak? If the vision is not communicated in a compelling way, then the organization is going to be unfocused. Wherever focus is lacking, only random activity is left. That's when you wake up and find you don't like the organization you're leading.[31]

Don't be surprised when people—even people on your leadership team—forget what's going on and drift back to old goals and familiar processes. In fact, expect your vision to leak, even in your own thoughts. Keep reinforcing the vision, keep pointing to the benefits, and don't let the inevitable setbacks stop you in your tracks.

---

31. "Vision Leaks," Andy Stanley, CT *Pastors*, Winter 2004, https://www.christianitytoday.com/pastors/2004/winter/andy-stanley-vision-leaks.html.

METHODS OF COMMUNICATION

We need to step back to take a look at how we've communicated vision in the past. Quite often, we'll find that the culture has moved at light speed, but we're still using horse-and-buggy methods. We need to tailor our methods of communication to the audience, using both high tech and high touch with deft skill. Customize it to the constituency. For instance, when we sit down with the board and other stakeholders, we want to be sure we're physically close enough to read each other's expressions. We want them to see the passion in our eyes and we want to see the response on their faces so we can explain more if they look puzzled, move on if they look bored, or use gentle but firm words if they appear to be resistant. When we talk to frontline employees or volunteers, we may give them something in writing, but again, we want to connect on a personal and emotional level. If they don't sense our desire and grasp the benefits to them, we've failed to connect in a meaningful way. We always communicate a blend of information and inspiration. Higher-level people—the board and the executive team—need far more information about the details and costs of the plan than frontline personnel and volunteers, but even those at the bottom of the organizational chart need enough information to give them confidence that we know what we're doing. We don't get into strategic and tactical conversations with salespeople and childcare volunteers, but the executive team must be involved in that level of talks for them to get excited about executing the plan.

> FOR EACH SPECIFIC AUDIENCE, LEADERS NEED TO COOK UP A DIFFERENT COMMUNICATION RECIPE—MORE MEAT FOR SOME, MORE SPICE FOR OTHERS.

For each specific audience, leaders need to cook up a communication recipe that's a little different from the others—more meat for some, more spice for others. Personal contact takes more time and energy, but we simply can't rely on platform addresses and polished presentations to connect with the hearts of those we need to share our vision. Speeches, written communication, an online presence, and spreadsheets can play their role, but they can never replace the power of people looking into our eyes in a one-on-one or small group setting. However, we don't have to cast the vision alone.

WHO, WHEN, HOW

Many leaders believe speaking to a large crowd is their most effective way to communicate vision and move people to participate. That's simply not the case. They will change more hearts by "cascading vision" from one tier to the other, speaking first to the stakeholders to get them onboard, then taking one or two of them to speak to the next tier, and taking a few of them to speak to the next, and so on until everyone in the business has heard from the leader in a small group context, with the active support of other leaders in the organization who also showed up to the meeting. Yes, this strategy of casting vision takes more time, but it pays far bigger dividends. It's the most productive way to address the *who, when,* and *how* of imparting vision. Many leaders don't want to hear it, but speaking from a platform has the lowest return on investment of any means of communicating vision. The larger the crowd, the lower the impact.

The leader's job is to create the vision, but even then, it can be a collaborative process. As I mentioned earlier, my strategy is to involve my executive team in the thinking and conceptualizing process. When I have a fresh idea and fledgling vision, I sit down with them, tell them my thoughts, and then I say, "I need your help. I need you to make this idea better." I don't ask, "Should we do this?" I don't ask, "Can we find the money and other resources to make it happen?" I don't ask, "How do you feel about it?" I don't ask, "Do you agree with this idea?" I don't open the door to doubts. Instead, I make them valued partners in crafting the very best possible plan to make the idea a reality. I use a whiteboard to write down their ideas with their name or initials next to each item. No idea is a bad idea; everything is considered. This validates their contribution, even though they know we can't do everything they suggest. This process is full of open dialogue so people feel free to voice their ideas and be creative. At some point, I begin asking them to explain how a particular idea might work, so they can explain the process and benefits of their concepts. Of course, a big vision requires many meetings to define the vision more clearly and think through the plans, benefits, and challenges, but this method shifts the burden of strategic thinking from one person's shoulders to the entire team.

In the cascade of communicating vision, there's one vision creator, the senior leader. He or she enlists the board, executive team, and key stakeholders to also become vision casters, so the organization has a cohesive and comprehensive voice. Everyone who sees the value in accomplishing the vision becomes vision carriers who talk it up to those around them. Caring about the vision is everyone's responsibility.

THE CASCADE OF COMMUNICATING VISION

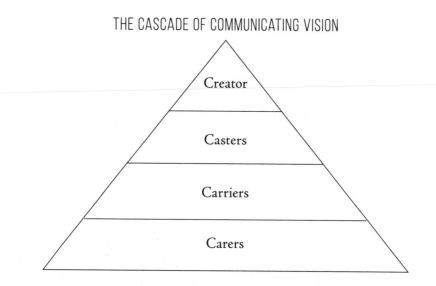

Leaders who are both secure and wise recognize that some of their executive team and other top leaders have great influence with certain audiences in the organization. Instead of being the only voice of the vision, these leaders enlist their lieutenants to either become the voice to those audiences or at least be a second voice to them. In this way, there are multiple vision casters, all speaking the same language with the same enthusiasm, but with slightly different ways of articulating the benefits and the process. This doesn't cause confusion. Quite the opposite—it creates synergy of leadership, vision, and passion.

Unfortunately, very few leaders have adopted this strategy of identifying influencers, enlisting them to be vision casters, and sending them to their target audiences. Too many of us rely exclusively on ourselves to communicate, inspire, and motivate others to action. Enlisting multiple vison casters isn't difficult; we simply need to identify the target groups, such as departments or branch offices, and then identify the leaders who have the most influence with these groups.

In conversations with leaders of large and successful organizations, several have told me they are very frustrated because people on their leadership teams don't do a good job casting vision. They either avoid even trying to paint a picture of the future, or they paint it in a way that has too many grays and not enough vibrant colors. I've encouraged these CEOs and presidents not to assume their senior leaders know how to cast vision clearly and compellingly. They need training and the CEOs and presidents need to train them. Each one needs a powerful script with illustrations so they know what to say. They need to practice their presentations in role plays and receive coaching so they can improve their communication skills. Companies don't send out people to sell products without training them in sales techniques. In the same way, they shouldn't expect senior leaders to be proficient in casting vision without first being trained. Casting vision may be second nature to the top leaders, but it isn't yet for the people on their teams.

> PART OF THE PLANNING PROCESS IS CREATING A STRATEGY OF MULTIPLYING VISION CASTERS AND PUTTING THEM IN POSITION TO BE EFFECTIVE.

Part of the planning process is creating a strategy of multiplying vision casters and putting them in position to be effective. I know a few leaders who do a fantastic job of gathering and equipping influencers for the causes they champion. They have spent time cultivating these relationships and the payoff is exponential. They wouldn't think of leading any other way. They meet with the influencers to share the vision and talk about how those people can communicate with individuals or groups. The leader explains the information and the benefits that will inspire their listeners and he preps them by talking about the questions and concerns they might encounter. When the influencers are prepared and engage those people, the vision cascades to another part of the organization.

Why don't most senior leaders use this communication strategy? Because their egos insist they be the center of attention and the sole voice of the vision.

I've seen some leaders make another major mistake in all three areas: who, when, and how. They first went to people who weren't in positions of authority because they were sure these people would get excited. Maybe they'd had resistance from their top leaders in the past so they were hesitant to go to them first. It's a huge mistake. Reverse cascading doesn't work! In many cases, though, there are no ulterior motives or hidden agendas. The leader is excited about a new idea and finds the first set of people who will listen. The problem, of course, is that the top-level leaders *feel* ignored and bypassed—because, however inadvertently, they *were* ignored and bypassed.

Most of the trouble in organizations comes from the third level of involvement. Usually, the executive team gets on board and is enthusiastic. The second level, the managers, are familiar with the process of implementing change, so they adopt and support the change. The third level people, the frontline employees in business, are the ones who are the most fragile. In many cases, that's where dissension begins, festers, and infects a large number of others before the top leader even is aware it's happening. This often occurs because the leader hasn't communicated well enough on their level and the fear of change is still greater than the desire to fulfill the vision. The leader hasn't created enough meaning for them; he hasn't articulated the objectives and key results, so the new goal does not move the person's heart, hands, and pocketbook.

IT HAS HAPPENED BEFORE

We see a cascade of communication of vision in Luke's account of the early church in Acts. Paul and Barnabas returned from their journey through the cities of what is now Turkey. (See Acts 14–15.) In each community, they first went to the Jewish synagogue to announce that Jesus was the Messiah. When they received a cold reception, they took the message to the Gentiles, who often were more receptive. When the two men returned to their base in Antioch, some people were upset that Paul had not required the Gentiles to be circumcised before starting churches among them.

Paul had a much larger vision because he had seen faith at work among the Gentiles. He realized this would exponentially expand the reach of the gospel far beyond the Jewish people. Paul could have ignored the men who resisted him, but he didn't bypass the established channels of authority. Instead, he reported details about the Gentiles' faith and miracles he performed in every city.

Paul's vision to admit Gentiles into the early church without a circumcision requirement had key stakeholder casters: Peter and James. Nothing was left to chance. The vision was carefully considered, fully vetted, and implemented with passion and skill. Letters and groups of disciples went out to spread the vision and inspiration everywhere. Soon, everyone cared about it.

This moment changed the course of history. Who knows what would have happened if this vision had not been implemented?

You and I can follow Paul's pattern of identifying a vision, crafting it, presenting it, enlisting influencers to join us in casting it, and seeing many others become enthusiastic carriers.

THINK ABOUT IT...

1. What does it mean that leaders must be bilingual? Which of the two languages, abstract or concrete, is your natural language?

2. What are some ways it helps to realize most of the people in our organization need to hear both languages from the beginning?

3. Review the "Seven Steps in Communicating Vision." Which of these do you do naturally? Which need some attention? How will you improve?

4. Describe the concept of "cascading vision." How would implementing this strategy be more effective than a one-person show?

5. Who are the influencers you can count on to be vision casters? What are their areas of influence?

6. What is one thing you need to do now to cast vision more clearly and powerfully?

10

HOW *DO I* MOTIVATE THOSE I LEAD?
THE QUESTION OF DISCOVERY

In my experience, there are two great motivators in life.
One is fear. The other is love.
You can manage an organization by fear, but if you do,
you will ensure that people won't perform up to their capabilities.
—Jan Carlson,
former chairman and CEO of Scandinavian Airlines

After I came to America, I enrolled in a Bible college. I was, by all measures, the most forgettable student on campus. My English wasn't very good, I wasn't the same skin color as anyone else, I wasn't a snappy dresser, and I wasn't exactly the most popular guy on campus. In my sophomore year, I attended a church near the school. The pastor, Tom Grinder, had a ritual before each service. He stayed in the lobby greeting people until about two minutes before it began. When he came in, he walked down the side of the church around the piano and up to the platform. When he sat down in his chair, it was the signal for the worship leader to stand for the first song. I always sat on the back row.

One week on a Thursday night, when Pastor Grinder walked by me, he tapped me on the shoulder, leaned over, and whispered, "Sam, pick up a hymnal. You're leading the singing tonight." He didn't stop for a reply. He kept walking up to the front.

I had never led singing in my life. I had never *thought about* leading singing in my life. At that moment, I was sure no one in his right mind would ever ask me to lead singing, but I knew that when Pastor Grinder sat down, somebody—I guess it was me—would be expected to stand up and lead the congregation in song. I grabbed a hymnal and raced to catch up with him. I didn't know many songs, but I remembered that number 57 was "Amazing Grace" and number 128 was "Victory in Jesus." I quickly walked over to Jean, who was playing the piano, and we picked a third song. Instantly, I went up to the podium and announced, "Welcome to you tonight. Turn to number 57 in your hymnals. We're going to begin with 'Amazing Grace.'"

My mind raced to remember everything the regular song leader did each week. I tried to copy him as much as possible, but I hadn't paid close attention in all the services I had attended. I hope I looked confident. I'd never done this before, but the people sitting in the pews didn't know I'd never done it before.

After the service, Pastor Grinder told me the regular song leader was sick that night. I probably prayed for his healing more fervently than I'd ever prayed before, but after all was said and sung, the singing had not gone too badly. In fact, Pastor Grinder asked me to substitute again a few times. Several weeks later, he came to me after church and said, "Sam, we have some choir robes in the back that we haven't used in years. Would you like to start a choir?"

I had never worn a choir robe, I had never been in a choir, and I'd certainly never led a choir, but I said, "Sure. I'd love to."

I asked a number of friends, including Brenda, who is now my wife, to join the choir. The robes were classic, green with gold trim, but they had a permanent crease where the hangers had held them for so many years. No problem. They were the best robes we'd ever worn. My robe had tailored sleeves so I could wave my arms without hurting anyone. We practiced and learned enough songs to perform. We must have been pretty good because we got a bus and went on the road to sing for other churches.

A few months later, Pastor Grinder came to me and asked, "Sam, how about starting a nursing home ministry?"

I had no idea what he meant. Was it a home for nurses? In those days, we didn't have nursing homes in India. Old people lived and died with their families. After he explained it to me, I said, "Sure, I'll do it."

I found a nursing home about eight miles from the campus. When I went there to talk to the administrator, I quickly discovered he was Jewish. I wasn't aware of any historical, cultural, or social tensions between Jews and Christians, so I just waded in to offer to bring people to sing for the people there and listen to them as they told stories about their lives. He agreed to let us come. I played the accordion and gathered my friends to join me in visiting the elderly people at the home. Before long, over a hundred people attended our gatherings.

I have no idea what Pastor Grinder saw in me, but he discovered hidden desires and talents that I didn't know existed. Before he tapped me on the shoulder that one Thursday night, I had lived in obscurity. To earn money to pay my tuition and board, I had been a breakfast cook, washed dishes, and cleaned bathrooms. But Pastor Grinder saw potential no one else noticed. Suddenly, I was leading singing with people in the congregation who ate the breakfasts I cooked, used the dishes I washed, and went to the bathrooms I cleaned.

DISCOVERED BY SOMEONE

All of us were discovered by someone at some point in our lives. No one is a self-made man or woman. One of our most important tasks as leaders is to discover people around us. But before we talk about them, let's talk about you. Who discovered you? Someone discovered the latent potential in Abraham Lincoln, Billy Graham, Mother Teresa, Bill Gates, and every other leader who has made an impact on others, whether these people have made headlines or not. When a teacher noticed we were good at math, writing, or history, she saw something perhaps no one had ever seen before. When a coach pushed us to play better, it was because he saw we could do more than we had expected. When an employer said "yes" to us when we were looking for a job, she was taking a chance to discover our potential.

The people who discovered us saw raw (and maybe deeply hidden) talent, took an interest in our growth and development, gave us opportunities to try our wings, and validated our unique way of thinking and serving.

In an article for *Forbes*, Glenn Llopis said this about leaders who discovered him:

> They each brought a unique perspective to my development and their wisdom pushed me to see things about my own leadership capabilities and aptitudes that I had never seen, fully appreciated or understood before.[32]

> THE PEOPLE WHO DISCOVERED US SAW RAW TALENT, GAVE US OPPORTUNITIES TO TRY OUR WINGS, AND VALIDATED OUR UNIQUE WAY OF THINKING AND SERVING.

Sometimes, people try to discover us, but we say, "No, not me, and not now." In 1997, John Maxwell had recently moved to Atlanta. His friends Bill McCartney of Promise Keepers and Pastor Jack Hayford told him, "You need to meet Sam." John came to my office, sat across the table, and told me his vision to develop leaders. He asked if I'd join him. I knew it would mean giving up my role as president of the Bible college, which was the biggest, most influential job I could imagine. I replied, "Thank you, John, but no, I'm not interested."

When I got home that night and told Brenda about the conversation, she instantly said something snarky about my lack of sanity. She told me, "You shouldn't have turned him down. You can do both." I hadn't thought of that.

A week later, John spoke at chapel at our school. After his message, he came to my office. I told him, "I don't want to leave where I'm serving now, but I think I can partner with you and support your vision. Let's talk about

---

32. "Leadership Is All About Enabling the Full Potential in Others," Glenn Llopis, *Forbes*, July 29, 2014, https://www.forbes.com/sites/glennllopis/2014/07/29/leadership-is-about-enabling-the-full-potential-in-others/#14b93e866698.

it again. Let me see what part is congruent with me and my abilities." At the time, John's vision had three components: building leaders internationally; in colleges and universities; and in urban settings. I told him I'd like to participate in building leaders in cities. It was, in many ways, the launching pad for the rest of my career. My first "no" was short-sighted. Thanks to Brenda, I thought about it more and found a way to say "yes."

THE PROCESS OF DISCOVERY

Great leaders are students of their people. They observe and study those who report to them so they can bring out the best in them. These leaders are always in the process of discovery. This shouldn't surprise anyone. If you're married, you know that you're continually finding out more about your spouse. You thought you had uncovered the depths of feelings, perspective, fears, and dreams, but you often realize you have more to learn… and for some of us, much more.

The people on our teams aren't just filling a slot and cranking out work. If that's the way we see them, we'll have little impact on their development and we won't tap into the best they have to offer. To lead our people well, we need to launch a process of discovery in three primary areas: their gifts, their passions, and their wavelengths.

DISCOVER THEIR GIFTS

We can look at a résumé to identify training, credentials, and experience, but these may not tell the whole story of a person's talents. We need to observe what activities are intuitive, what brings delight, and what seems to take little effort. The list is endless. Some people are terrifically insightful about others, some can figure out systems in the blink of an eye, some have amazing musical talents, some are physically strong, some are visionaries, some are meticulous, some have a knack for numbers, and on and on. I know some people who make a point of differentiating spiritual gifts and natural talents. We don't need to get into that debate, but I'd only say that every ability we possess is a gift from God.

Why do leaders need to help some people discover their talents? First, people need validation. Like teenagers, they've tried a dozen different things to see if any of them stick, but they're not sure what they can do well. Leaders can step in, notice strengths, and point them out. Validation is one of the most powerful and important messages leaders can communicate to their people. Second, it helps the leader know how to place people where they can thrive and contribute their best to the organization. When a leader discovers and points out a team member's talents, everybody wins.

DISCOVER THEIR PASSIONS

> WHAT KEEPS YOUR PEOPLE UP AT NIGHT WITH BIG DREAMS AND HIGH HOPES? WHAT CAN THEY NOT STOP THINKING ABOUT?

Occasionally, a person may be very talented in an area but lacks passion, or even lacks interest. This problem is not as rare as you might think. I know some people who have remarkable mental acuity in math, but they work in areas where they seldom need it. They're more interested in people, systems, or leadership. They amaze their family and friends by their ability to almost instantly figure out the day of the week a year away or the total of two large numbers multiplied, but they're indifferent about that ability.

What are your people *passionate* about? What *drives* them? What keeps them up at night with big dreams and high hopes? What makes their eyes light up? What makes their hearts beat faster? What can they *not* stop thinking about? What elicits tears and laughter? What makes them stay longer to figure out the next step? What is so important that they defend it against all those who doubt them? The thing at the center of these responses is their *reason for living*.

DISCOVER THEIR WAVELENGTHS

All of the people in our lives, including family and friends, are positioned somewhere on a frequency, like a radio picking up a certain station. If Brenda is on FM and I'm thinking and talking on AM, she won't hear a word I say. And if I go to FM, but I'm on a different station, she still won't hear me.

We can tune in to our people by turning the dial from telling to asking to emotional connections. Too often, leaders walk into a meeting with an agenda in hand and begin wading through the items. Their goal is to download the information and directions as efficiently as possible so they can go on to the next meeting. Some of the people are on their wavelength, but at least a few probably aren't. Maybe they didn't sleep last night, maybe their baby was sick, maybe they're worried about finances or health or something else, or maybe another person said something offensive just before the meeting started. Whatever the cause, these people aren't listening. The first solution is to ask questions. This helps you determine who's on your wavelength and who isn't. It also helps you get on the wavelength of those who are distracted for any reason. It's vital for all of us to acquire the skill of asking great questions.

In some cases, the questions bring up hurt, fear, or anger that can't be adequately addressed in the meeting. If leaders just keep wading through their agenda, they may communicate that they don't really care. Another way to handle this situation is to say, "I want to talk with you about that after the meeting." Then, in a different setting, the leader can get on the emotional wavelength of the person, show-

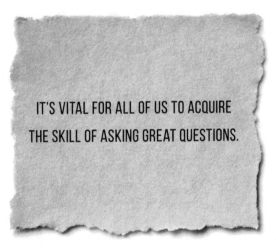

IT'S VITAL FOR ALL OF US TO ACQUIRE THE SKILL OF ASKING GREAT QUESTIONS.

ing compassion, seeking to understand more than to direct. In these cases, empathy is the best source of resolution.

For some teams, the leader needs to walk in and give crystal-clear directions. That's exactly what's needed. But for most teams, the leader should say, "Here's my idea. Make it better," or "That event went really well. What can we do even better next time?" If a group has been together for a while, they often have a collective wavelength. In many cases, the team picks up the leader's emotional frequency and reflects that optimism or pessimism, delight or apathy.

Leaders who are students of their people learn how to get on their wavelength intellectually and conceptually, tailoring their vocabulary and the complexity of their concepts to fit the capacity of the group. They also discover the relational maturity so they'll know whether to expect their team members to act like teenagers or adults. The illustrations and expectations of the leader are also shaped by the socio-economic wavelength of the people in the room.

The receptivity of each person is greatly affected by past and current events. As we've seen, a history of painful relationships may make some defiant, but it makes others too compliant. And current problems at home can make it very difficult for team members to focus on the job at hand.

In all of these, the leader doesn't look at the challenges and give up on making progress. Instead, great leaders notice when people aren't on their frequency and they ask questions and make compassionate connections to get on the same wavelength as their people. If you want people to give everything they've got to your organization and your cause, make sure they feel like you're both tuned to the same station.

TAKE THE TIME TO BUILD YOUR BEST CULTURE

Some people in the business world might insist, "I don't have time for all this. We have work to do!" I would respectfully suggest that discovering your team's gifts, passions, and wavelengths will help you create a culture that will get far more work accomplished. In their book, *A Better Way*, entrepreneurs Randall Keene and Timothy McKibben assert:

> Culture has a profound impact on people and shapes the processes they use. If a leader creates a dysfunctional culture, the equipment isn't affected, but the people suffer. The company's overall culture is always—always—a reflection of the purpose and personality of the president. A strong and healthy culture can be a tremendous fuel for success by creating an environment that inspires creativity, cooperation, and self-improvement, but only if the president values

those traits in leading the management team. It starts at the top, and it's sustained by perpetual, intentional effort from the top.[33]

Leaders need to discover the gifts, passions, and wavelengths of the people who are their direct reports—that's where culture is created and that's where it's sustained. But these leaders also need to interact in meaningful ways with people beyond their teams. GE CEO Jack Welsh described this as "management by walking around." It's important to get out of our offices and conference rooms to rub shoulders with people down the chain of command, to notice, at least to some degree, what they do exceptionally well, what they're excited about, and what station they're tuned to. Pastors can take time to talk to greeters, childcare workers, sound and light technicians, and choir members. Business leaders can talk to the people in the call center, sales, marketing, and production. Just showing up to be seen and to listen is half the battle—maybe more. People want to work in a place where they feel valued and the attentive presence of a leader communicates value.

PEOPLE WANT TO WORK IN A PLACE WHERE THEY FEEL VALUED AND THE ATTENTIVE PRESENCE OF A LEADER COMMUNICATES VALUE.

Churches and businesses motivate people in very similar ways. The only real difference is how they measure success. In business, success is usually monetized in revenues, profits, and share price. Every new business starts with the question: how do we make money from this idea? The church measures things like souls saved, people in groups, and the number of missionaries. Budgets and buildings are means to those ends. Businesses and churches have more in common than many people think: they both make financial, staffing, facility, liability, and legal decisions; they both have stakeholders and some form of

33. Randall Keene and Timothy McKibben, *A Better Way* (Friendswood, Texas: Baxter Press, 2016), 128.

organizational hierarchy; both can grow and thrive; and both can be split by disgruntled people who take other disgruntled people with them.

BECOME A TRANSFORMATIONAL LEADER

My friend Stephen Fogarty earned his Ph.D. by doing research on how pastors can become transformational leaders. The principles in his book, *Light a Fire*, apply beyond the church to nonprofits and businesses, too. He identifies four primary characteristics of transformational leadership:

IDEALIZED INFLUENCE

To have an impact on those who follow, leaders must be attractive. Their characters must have a blend of boldness and humility, kindness and tenacity. When leaders lose the respect of those around them, people spend most of their time protecting themselves, promoting themselves, or looking for an escape hatch to bail out.

INSPIRATIONAL MOTIVATION

Great leaders have the innate gifts, or perhaps the acquired skill, to craft a message to capture hearts and redirect lives. To them, words aren't stale and lifeless; they have enormous power to inspire, correct, and transform individuals, groups, and communities. Ronald Reagan, Winston Churchill, Nelson Mandela, and Martin Luther King, Jr. are stirring examples of people who understood how to shape their messages to move people to action.

INTELLECTUAL STIMULATION

Gifted leaders ask piercing questions and offer novel perspectives. When they speak or write, others often wonder, *Why didn't I think of that?* The messages of these leaders push people to think more deeply, to wrestle with facts and ideas, and to shape their lives around a new way of looking at truth.

INDIVIDUALIZED CONSIDERATION

Leaders are effective because they touch a few who become infected with the same enthusiasm and subsequently infect many others. A great speaker may make a dent in the masses, but the best leaders know they need to focus on the few. Virtually all revolutionary movements were begun by individual leaders who captured the imagination of a small group of men and women. The followers became enamored with the leader's power, certainty, determination, and, in some cases, humility and compassion.

JESUS WAS A MODEL LEADER

Stephen points out that the leader who exemplifies these traits most perfectly is Jesus. Jesus can be our model, our example, and our guide as we seek to motivate people on our teams. In his book, Stephen writes that some pastors—and, by extension, leaders in other fields—are long on vision, but short on practical steps to get there. Others have exemplary characters, but they don't provide much of a spark to inflame the motivation of others. Few leaders, Stephen notes, stimulate deep reflection in their people. In other words, most leaders don't equip people to think.

He writes about Christ:

Jesus continually challenged His listeners' normal way of thinking about God and life. Over and over again, people had to think more deeply about what He said so they could understand it and apply it, and the disciples often asked Him to explain His points.

Then Stephen asks us:

How often do people ask us to explain more of what we've said—and do they ask because it's particularly insightful and challenging or because our point has been so opaque that no one could grasp it? Don't be intellectually lazy. Find authors and teachers who stretch your mind and heart. Dive into their books and sermons, wrestle with their points, and find ways to adapt their teaching in your own messages.[34]

We can't just assume people around us "should" be motivated because we are or because they're paid to do a job. We have to think more deeply and more clearly about what lights their fire. As we validate their talents, inspire and direct their passions, and get on their wavelengths, we'll create

---

34. Stephen Fogarty, *Light a Fire* (Parramatta, NSW: Australasian Pentecostal Studies, 2016), 49–53.

a culture of dogged optimism, vibrant creativity, and undying hope. Aren't those the kind of people you want to lead?

THINK ABOUT IT...

1. Who discovered you? How did it happen? What was the impact on you?

2. Think about the people who report to you and answer these questions for each one:

   › What are three things the person does well?

   › What causes this person to sit up and get excited?

   › What is this person's wavelength?

3. On a scale of 0 (not at all) to 10 (really well) how well do you know your people? Or better yet, how well do they think you know them? Explain your answer.

4. How can you leverage these insights about your team to maximum effect?

5. What kind of culture are you creating? How can you ask better questions and get on their emotional frequency more often?

6. If you had applied the principles and practices in this chapter two years ago, how would your team and your organization be different today?

7. How would you rate yourself in the four areas of transformational leadership? What's your strength? What could use some attention?

11

WHAT IS IT ABOUT ME THAT'LL KEEP ME FROM BECOMING ALL I'M DESTINED TO BE? THE QUESTION OF GROWTH

You are never too old to set another goal or dream a new dream.
—C.S. Lewis

There's one question I ask myself every day—and often ten times in a day. It's the question that if I fail to ask and answer it, my life will soon be stuck with little growth and far less to offer others. You could say I'm obsessed with this question, but I don't think there's anything wrong with this intensity. In fact, I believe all of us should be obsessed with it. The question I continually ask myself is, "What is it about *me* that'll keep *me* from becoming all I'm destined to be?" Or to put it in a kingdom perspective, "What is it about *me* that'll keep *me* from becoming all that God intends for *me* to be?"

Some leaders don't want to ask this question because it focuses on them and they feel uncomfortable in the spotlight. Maybe these leaders have emotional baggage from past failures they don't want to unlock and open. Maybe they're assuming there's nothing to evaluate. Maybe they think they're too busy doing all kinds of "more important" things. Whatever the reason, the lack of self-evaluation prevents them from making thousands of mid-course corrections and taking advantage of growth opportunities.

Again and again, I take a hard look at how I respond to Brenda, how I react to something people on our team say or do, my flippancy over a matter that's really important to someone, whether I'm fully present in a conversation or I'm drifting off thinking about something else, or any other yellow flag that calls for my attention. If I catch them when they are mild warnings, they won't become catastrophes.

ASK THE TOUGH PERSONAL QUESTIONS

I know plenty of inquisitive leaders, men and women, who ask great questions so they can think more clearly, but most of these people are riveted on improving their organizations, not their personal growth. I encourage them to be their own personal trainer and ask:

- What are three changes I can make today that will pay dividends in my life in the next six months? (What hindrances need to be addressed and eliminated? What good things can be accelerated?)

- How can I improve as a spouse, child, sibling, and parent?

- What season of life am I in? What should be happening in this season?

- How can I prepare for the next season of my life?

- Who is the friend or mentor who is on speed dial when my life is on fire and I need help immediately?

- When I need help with a process in my organization, who do I trust for advice and support?

- How am I building my most important relationships today so that when I'm dead, at least those people will remember and miss me?

I'm not suggesting these are easy or fun questions to ponder, but I believe they are essential if leaders are going to fulfill their highest potential. For me, part of this process is to ask those close to me what they see in me. Self-deception is a chronic disease for all of us. We're wise to ask people we trust for honest—if sometimes brutal—feedback.

Some people might wonder if focusing on our growth is selfish. No, I don't believe it's selfish at all. It's required, especially if we're serious about following God. Rigorous self-evaluation is a necessary path toward humility, obedience, and usefulness. The Scriptures say quite a lot about its importance. Here are only a few examples from the New Testament:

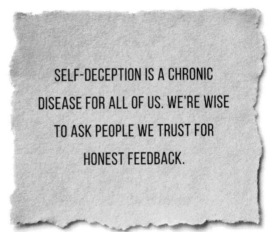

SELF-DECEPTION IS A CHRONIC DISEASE FOR ALL OF US. WE'RE WISE TO ASK PEOPLE WE TRUST FOR HONEST FEEDBACK.

+   Jesus famously warned us, "*Why do you look at the speck of sawdust in your brother's eye and pay no attention to the plank in your own eye? How can you say to your brother, 'Let me take the speck out of your eye,' when all the time there is a plank in your own eye? You hypocrite, first take the plank out of your own eye, and then you will see clearly to remove the speck from your brother's eye*" (Matthew 7:3–5).

+   Paul insists on a well-examined life: "*Do not conform to the pattern of this world, but be transformed by the renewing of your mind. Then you will be able to test and approve what God's will is—his good, pleasing and perfect will*" (Romans 12:2).

+   In a sobering invitation to take a hard look at our hearts, Paul told the Corinthians, "*Examine yourselves to see whether you are in the faith; test yourselves. Do you not realize that Christ Jesus is in you—unless, of course, you fail the test?*" (2 Corinthians 13:5).

+   James warns that we can hear God's word but fail to let it change us: "*Do not merely listen to the word, and so deceive yourselves. Do what it says. Anyone who listens to the word but does not do what it says is like someone who looks at his face in a mirror and, after looking at himself, goes away and immediately forgets what he looks like*" (James 1:22–24).

In an article for *Christianity Today*, Alannah Francis compares necessary reflection to medical and dental checkups:

> As Christians, self-assessment becomes an increasingly important part of our faith as we grow and mature spiritually. Just as periodic checkups with doctors and dentists help us take care of our physical health, regular reflection on how we're performing in accordance with our faith and what steps we need to take to remedy any areas of weakness helps us become stronger spiritually. It also enables us to tackle problems before they become out of control. God encourages us to look inward in order to identify areas of weakness so that we can address them.[35]

A big part of our penchant for self-deception is the natural desire to blame others for our errors and faults. We want to point the finger at someone else—anyone else—so we don't have to do the hard work of recalibrating our lives. I've had to come to the conclusion that only one person can prevent me from becoming the person God wants me to be. It's not my parents, or Brenda, or people on my team, or those who have been less than honest or loyal during the course of my life. The only one who can block my path is *me*. If I let past hurts or present disappointments stop me, I've given them power I should reserve for myself. I'm responsible to walk with God and trust Him to change me, place me, and use me in any way He chooses.

CONTINUAL IMPROVEMENT

I carry the weight of responsibility to lead my organization and my team, but I'm not alone. I continually ask:

+ What or who do I need so I can grow and develop?

+ Who can step into my life to support me as I answer these questions?

+ Who can be my coach to help me take the next steps?

All of us need somebody. It's not an option. I know a leader who has formed a group to meet with him once a month and he has asked them

---

35. "8 Bible verses on the importance of self-examining your spiritual life," Alannah Francis, *Christianity Today*, June 22, 2016, https://www.christiantoday.com/article/8-bible-verses-on-the-importance-of-self-examining-your-spiritual-life/88893.htm.

to give him feedback on the questions asked in this chapter. He picked these people because they each have two qualities: they're wise and they're devoted to him. He trusts that they don't have another agenda, so their input is free from hidden expectations and manipulation. He tells them what's on his heart and what questions he's wrestling with, and he says, "Talk to me. Give me your honest impressions. You won't hurt my feelings. And if it does hurt my feelings, I'll let you know right now so we can process the pain together. I trust you." For him, this meeting is a greenhouse of growth.

Most leaders, I suspect, secretly prefer the emotional and personal distance created by their position of leadership. Distance makes them feel at least somewhat immune from feedback. After all, they've gotten plenty of negative and undeserved feedback over the years, so emotional isolation feels safer than being exposed. I'm not recommending being vulnerable to everyone we know. We need just a few who have those two qualities of wisdom and loyalty. You can feel safe with them, safe enough to stop being Superman or Wonder Woman and be vulnerable.

I speak to many thousands of people every year, but there are few people who are close enough and bold enough to tell me, "Sam, that was a good talk, but you might think about shortening the opening and I'd consider adding a point under heading number 3." When people do that for me, I know they're really paying attention, they're thinking deeply, and they care enough about me to give me honest feedback.

RAISE THE CEILING

Continual improvement raises the ceiling in every area we address. If I bring a helium balloon into a room in my house and let it go, it rises only to the ceiling. If it's an eight-foot ceiling, that's as far as it can go. But if I call a renovation company to come to my house and raise the ceiling to twelve feet, I'll invest time and money and it'll be a mess for a while, but the balloon can rise higher than before. Let me ask: What are you doing to raise your ceiling?

+ If your role requires you to be an expert in communication, what are three resources you've recently utilized to improve your skills?

- If you're a CEO or a pastor, what are three books you've recently read or conferences you've attended that have refreshed your vision and given you new ideas?

- If you're a project administrator, what are the last three tools you've used to hone your talents and make you more effective?

- If your job is in marketing, what are three creative, innovative, cutting-edge concepts you've seen or read about recently?

- If your role is administrative assistant, what are three new types of software, tips, or techniques that you've recently used to make you more efficient?

- If you're a team leader or a department manager, what are three insights you've gained in the past couple of months from books or articles that have helped you be a better leader?

- If you have a family, what are three recent books, blogs, articles, or podcasts that have sharpened your ability to love your spouse and children well?

You may ask, "Why do you frame all those questions as 'recently' or 'in the past couple of months'?" I put it that way because if you have to think very long and hard about only three things you've done to improve your talents, you're not doing enough to raise your ceiling!

All of nature tends toward randomness; scientists call it *entropy*. Our companies and churches can't be all they can be if we don't continually inject meaning and order, and organizations easily lose focus when leaders don't stay sharp. Comfort isn't the aim of great leaders. They are wise to ask themselves some pointed questions. An article titled "10 Smart Questions that Challenge the Drift toward Irrelevance" suggests these:

1. "What are we afraid to say out loud?" In what ways are we and members of our team engaged in intentional blindness?

2. "If we fail to achieve our goal, what will we not have done?" What are the holes in the planning process?

3. "What assumptions drive our decisions?" Including assumptions about the future, the markets, our people, etc.

4. "If we were replaced tomorrow, what would the new team do?" Think like you're fresh on the job.

5. "Who is underutilized?" Who has talents but isn't using them, for whatever reason?

6. "What are we doing that isn't working as well as it used to?" What processes need to be improved and which ones need to be scrapped?

7. "What results best fulfill our vision and justify our existence?" What metrics really matter?

8. "If we couldn't fail, what would we do next?" What's the "blue sky" dream for the company or organization?

9. "How might we create our own frustrations?" What systems reduce tension and which ones cause more problems than they solve?

10. "What's the easiest thing we could do today to move the ball forward?" Think creatively and strategically: what single decision can have the biggest impact?[36]

These questions prod us to look more intently, see more clearly, think more perceptively, and be ruthlessly honest so we can reverse the slide toward irrelevance. As we address them, we'll almost certainly see that we need to make some changes and acquire new skills so we can stay on top of our changing culture.

NEW COMPETENCIES

Alvin Toffler, the author of *Future Shock*, commented, "The illiterate of the twenty-first century will not be those who cannot read and write, but those who cannot learn, unlearn, and relearn." When we raise the ceiling, we'll need new furniture to match the scale. Similarly, when an organization grows, the CEO must acquire new skills to lead a larger, more complex system. Some who were nurturers in the early stages when there was only a roomful of employees need to learn to be gatherers and expand the room to fit more people.

---

36. "10 Smart Questions that Challenge the Drift toward Irrelevance," *Leadership Freak*, June 25, 2016, https://leadershipfreak.blog/2016/06/25/10-smart-questions-that-challenge-the-drift-toward-irrelevance.

It's much harder to unlearn than to learn. When I was younger, I taught myself a number of musical instruments, including saxophone, guitar, keyboard, and accordion. I didn't have enough money for lessons, so I just watched others and tried my best to emulate them. Years later when I could afford professional lessons, I had an exceptionally hard time unlearning the finger patterns I'd used for many years. I taught myself to play golf and my swing today is much like it was at the beginning. Lessons haven't helped much. No matter how hard my instructor tried, my muscle memory fought against me. That's not an excuse for mediocrity, but this truth forms a reasonable expectation for the difficulty of changing habits of a lifetime.

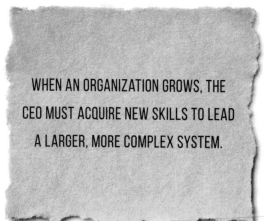

WHEN AN ORGANIZATION GROWS, THE CEO MUST ACQUIRE NEW SKILLS TO LEAD A LARGER, MORE COMPLEX SYSTEM.

As a part of our evaluation of competencies, we'll need to enhance those that are productive and propel us into the future and eliminate those that don't. A few years ago, as I thought about my future, I quickly realized I needed to enhance my ability to train leaders, my writing skills, and my speaking ability. Anything that competed with these priorities needed to be weeded out of my priority list. I don't speak at women's gatherings, men's meetings, or marriage retreats...unless a dear friend leans on me. I'm narrowing my "yes" replies and broadening the "no" ones. It's not easy, but it's necessary.

Elimination is essential to growth. You have to give up to go up. You can't steal second base by keeping your foot constantly on first. Columbus had to lose sight of Spain so he could find the New World.

ELIMINATING CLUTTER AND COOKIES

A few years ago, my computer unexpectedly (and very frustratingly) slowed to a crawl. I called someone to fix it. When he came, he asked me a strange question: "When was the last time you defragged your computer?"

I thought he was cursing, but he didn't look angry at all. "De what?" I asked.

He laughed. "I guess that means never."

I nodded. I was about to get a lesson. He explained, "It's like me walking into your closet and seeing all your pants, shirts, suits, belts, and shoes all over the place. Defragging puts all the white shirts together on hangers, all the blue shirts in one place, all the pants hung neatly in their spot, all the suits in one area, the belts on their hangers, and the shoes neatly arranged on the floor. Everything in its place."

I understood. He started running some diagnostic programs. After a while, he looked at me and made another strange comment: "You have too many cookies." I then had my second lesson of the day about websites leaving cookies on my computer so they can keep track of how I use their sites and customize pages. They are, in effect, memories of where we've been on the Internet. He defragged my computer and deleted the cookies.

In every interaction every moment of the day, people leave "cookies" in our minds and hearts. These are comments, gestures, and facial expressions that stick in the inner workings of our souls. They can leave positive and encouraging messages, or they may leave a hint (or more than a hint) of doubt or fear. If we don't defrag our minds and remove the negative messages, these things build up and cause all kinds of problems. One or two don't do much damage, but tens or hundreds or thousands of them, unrecognized and left alone, can ruin more than our day!

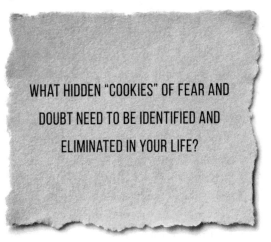

WHAT HIDDEN "COOKIES" OF FEAR AND DOUBT NEED TO BE IDENTIFIED AND ELIMINATED IN YOUR LIFE?

What hidden "cookies" of fear and doubt need to be identified and eliminated in your life? Be ruthless in analyzing your life and career to see what needs to be enhanced and what needs to be removed or defragged so you can be all you're destined to be.

LOOKING BACK, LOOKING FORWARD

As we think about what might prevent us from fulfilling our destinies, it's helpful to take a look at our past to see how important decisions have shaped our lives. Someone suggested I identify the most significant turning points in my life. We are, the person explained, the products of these few, perhaps four or five, decisions. In one way or another, everything we've become and everything we've done hinge on these few crucial choices. When I remember my thoughts and feelings around these events, I have more perspective to think clearly about the decisions I need to make in the future. I'm the product of four pivotal decisions:

1. Migrating to the United States

2. My decision to marry Brenda

3. Accepting the offer to become president of a Christian college, which became a university

4. Resigning from the university to pursue a full-time career in leadership development

The trajectory of our lives has been shaped by very few, but very important decisions. If any of them had been different, our lives would be on an altered path. We may look back on most of these moments with fondness and gratitude, but we may have mixed feelings about some of them. Still, they opened doors and closed doors. They put us in relationships with people who mean the most to us and they demanded we learn the hardest lessons of our lives. These lessons, crafted in the furnace of hardship as well as in the sunlit lands of our greatest joys, have propelled us forward to find more meaning than we could have imagined when we were young.

WHAT IF?

Ironically, one of the most common questions that clouds the thinking of leaders and prevents them from being "fully present" in their roles is inordinate fear about their future. Most of them don't have any solid plans about what will happen when they step out of their roles and the absence of a plan creates confusion and distractions. Worries about the future consume their thinking and they don't enjoy those last years because they live with chronic, low-grade worries. What we think about, we bring about, and what we obsess about, we imagine—whether it be a glorious future or a painful one.

Every leader needs to anticipate two types of succession events: planned and catastrophic. Wise leaders start looking at their transition years before they plan to retire or move on to another career. Many leaders, especially those who planted a church or founded a company and have seen it grow over many years, refuse to even think about leaving. They stick around longer than they are capable and the organization declines in their last years. Don't let that happen to you and your organization!

A succession plan has benchmarks, timelines, narratives, assignments, and specific levels of engagement and disengagement. Don't wait until your board or your staff force you to think about succession. Begin working on a plan many years ahead, look for exemplary leaders within your organization, and be involved in recruiting top talent. The best legacy you can leave your organization is to orchestrate a smooth transition of power. This plan is far better for your mental health, for your family, for your staff, for the new leader, and for everyone who benefits from what your organization offers.

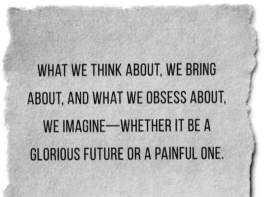

WHAT WE THINK ABOUT, WE BRING ABOUT, AND WHAT WE OBSESS ABOUT, WE IMAGINE—WHETHER IT BE A GLORIOUS FUTURE OR A PAINFUL ONE.

In an article on "Effective Onboarding: How to Introduce New Leadership to a Team," Robin Ahn gives helpful suggestions for a change of leadership. She recommends an overlapping transition period in which the new CEO serves under the existing leader for a period of time, perhaps a year. This gives people in the organization time to get to know the new leader and allows for a graceful exit by the one who is leaving. Ahn recommends the new hire realize key staff members may be resistant to change; in fact, they may harbor fears that the new leader may not appreciate them. A longer transition period provides time to build relationships, talk through roles and expectations, and calm anxieties. During this time, the new leader can clearly articulate expectations and metrics of success—for the organization, for each department, and for each person on the leadership team. Ahn points to a number of companies that crafted a plan for the first hundred days. One new CEO said he planned to meet with ten people in sales and ten major customers to get a better read on customer service.

> **THE BEST LEGACY YOU CAN LEAVE YOUR ORGANIZATION IS TO ORCHESTRATE A SMOOTH TRANSITION OF POWER.**

Ahn concludes:

> Finding the right leadership for your business [or church] is a big challenge and getting them adjusted to your corporate culture isn't always easy. However, these are not insurmountable tasks. Many companies not only survive, but thrive when new leadership is brought in.[37]

But sometimes, leaders suffer catastrophes: sudden health problems, accidents, moral failures, doctrinal deviance, and any other unexpected event that effectively takes the person out of a leadership role. Of course, no one wants to think about a sudden cessation of leadership, but wise leaders think about this when it seems very unlikely, like now. Spend some time with your board and senior leaders to craft a tentative plan for the unknown. It's like a couple having a last will and testament—they're not planning to die any time soon, but they've prepared for their children no matter what happens. I tell leaders that the only ones who don't need a catastrophic succession plan are those who know exactly when they're going to suffer a catastrophe. They get the sarcasm of that statement and I hope it moves them to action.

---

37. "Effective Onboarding: How to Introduce New Leadership to a Team," Robin Ahn, Workology, October 17, 2016, https://workology.com/effective-onboarding-how-to-introduce-new-leadership-to-a-team.

ALWAYS ASK GREAT QUESTIONS

I've noticed that great leaders invariably ask great questions. As we come to the close of how to think more clearly and effectively, consider at least some of the best questions I've read from outstanding leaders:

+ What trophy do we want on our mantle?

+ How can we become the company that would put us out of business?

+ In the past few months, what is the smallest change that has produced the biggest positive result?

+ What counts that we're not counting?

+ Are we paying enough attention to the partners our organization depends on to succeed?

+ What prevents me from making the changes I need to make to become a better leader?

+ Are we keeping up with the changes in the world around us? How can we tell?

+ If no one ever found out about my accomplishments, would it affect how I lead?

+ How likely is it that a customer or visitor will recommend us?

+ What is one word we want to stick in the minds of our customers, employees, and partners?

+ What should we stop doing?

+ If our board fired me and brought in a new CEO, what would the new person do differently?

+ What did we miss in the interview in the worst hire we've ever made?

+ How is the way I think and process information affecting our organizational culture?

+ Do we say "no" to customers for no reason?

+ Why should people listen to me?

+ What successful activity today is blinding us to new growth opportunities?

+ How do I encourage people to take more responsibility?[38]

BE ALL YOU CAN BE

Inspiring leaders push me to think better. Only if I think better can I climb higher, dive deeper, and have a more profound impact on the people around me. At the end of this book, I'm not going to give you three steps to do this or that. I only want to invite you to join me in the pursuit of clearer, more expansive thinking. For the rest of your life, I encourage you to:

+ Question your assumptions.

+ Challenge your certainties.

+ Ask second and third questions.

+ Embrace ambiguity and the process of change.

+ Teach people these principles.

---

38. These questions were adapted from "100 Great Questions Every Entrepreneur Should Ask," Leigh Buchanan, *Inc.*, March 31, 2014, https://www.inc.com/magazine/201404/leigh-buchanan/100-questions-business-leaders-should-ask.html.

THINK ABOUT IT...

1. How comfortable are you with self-evaluation? Would your spouse or best friend say you're comfortable with self-evaluation? Explain your answer.

2. What are three things you've been doing (or need to do) to raise the ceiling of your leadership?

3. What talents do you need to enhance by finding a coach or other resources? What difference will this make in your life and your career?

4. What do you need to defrag?

5. What are your four or five most significant decisions? How have they shaped your life's trajectory?

6. No matter how long you've been in your role, what are your planned and catastrophic succession plans? What will you do to fine-tune them?

7. What can you do to learn to ask better questions?

8. What have you learned from this book? How will you apply those lessons?

APPENDIX:
STAFF USER'S MANUAL

TO RELATE EFFECTIVELY TO PASTOR ROB KETTERLING
RIVER VALLEY CHURCH

*[This is the instrument Pastor Rob uses to help his staff
understand him and communicate more effectively with him.
Use it as an example and adapt it in any way that works for you and
the people who relate to you.]*

THIS IS HOW I THINK:

Everything is possible. I'm optimistic. I think the best is yet to come.

My mind is always thinking about all different sorts of things and in all different sorts of directions.

I think multitask, multifaceted, and multiple angles. I realize more is involved than what I see.

I love to think in the way of "Possibility – Why not? – Perhaps God – Let's do it!"

Stop making excuses, and let's make something happen!

I think ahead. I have to be ahead of the team because I'm the leader.

I think in segments: right now, today, this week, this month, this year, next ten years.

THIS IS HOW I LIKE THINGS DONE:

I like things done on time, with excellence, and with an added twist. I like things done with an extra added value and intentionality.

HOW DO YOU GIVE NEW IDEAS WITHOUT KNOCKING DOWN PREVIOUS IDEAS?

Use two words, "What if?"

If you say, "I'm not sure this is the best way to do it," that leads to defensiveness.

Bring me several possibilities. Are there more possibilities to the way we are doing something? Expand our thinking!

Also use the words, "How about . . . ?"

Let's open it up and make it better, not knock what was.

I believe that having lots of possibilities means we're all trying to make it better.

When you bring an idea to the people, you need to show the problem first so they know we need a solution.

When you bring an idea to me, you need to show me the possibilities first.

HOW DO YOU PROMOTE PEOPLE?

I promote people…

…when I get a full feedback loop.

…when I observe them doing well, their leaders say they are doing well, their peers say they are doing well, and their followers say they are doing well.

…when I recognize a gifting with the right time and an opportunity.

When all these factors come together quickly, we can expedite the promotion.

Some people think that all they have to do is kiss up to the leader, but that will not get you a promotion.

Some people are promoted by faithfulness, and a position opening up can give them an opportunity.

HOW DO YOU MEASURE AND DEFINE SUCCESS?

I measure success by results. But I have to be careful that this doesn't cause me to overlook character deficiencies. I have sometimes overlooked character deficiencies in skilled, effective people. In the long term, I need to see results paired with wholeness.

I measure success by the number of people you are taking on the journey. If you churn through staff and volunteers, that's a real concern for me. Show me you have time to breathe and grow because of all the people who are helping you.

I measure success in longevity—not just that you survived, but that you were thriving in your tenure.

I measure success by people doing what they are supposed to do.

Success is in the "yes!" Did you say "yes" and fulfill the "yes"?

Success is not in the number, but in the "yes."

Success is the pipeline of leaders under you.

I want you to stay for four years. I hope you will stay ten, and I would love it if you stayed a lifetime.

PEOPLE I PAY ATTENTION TO:

Whoever is helping us carry the load. I'm not going to pay attention to you if you aren't going to help us carry the load. You can carry it financially, through leadership, or through service.

I want to give attention to the people who are lifting this load!

If I have a free night, I want to give it to the people who are leading and lifting.

WHAT'S IMPORTANT TO YOU?

Honesty and loyalty—every leader wants loyalty. You can ask questions, but judge your spirit before asking. Ask in a right spirit.

There is no such thing as a "throw-away line." Anything you say is coming from somewhere in your heart.

I don't like surprises. If there's information I need (Big Info), I would rather know now than be surprised by finding out later.

HOW TO RELATE TO MY FAMILY:

I told the church early on, "You can forget my birthday, but don't forget my wife Becca's birthday!" I answered the call of God to do this church. If anyone disrespects my family, it catches my attention and my defenses come up.

I want people to honor my family, but I wouldn't like it to be flattery and appeasement. I look for authentic honor.

Whenever you are talking about my family, you can't "un say" what you said—so be careful!

I pray that I would never be the one to wink at sin in my family like Eli did with his boys, Hophni and Phineas.

If you are bringing me an issue about my family, keep it as closed a circle as possible. Let's try to deal with this and not spread gossip and misinformation.

Honor Becca for her sacrifice.

HOW WOULD YOU WANT SOMEONE ON STAFF TO TELL YOU THEY WANT TO START A CHURCH?

We are in an environment where we don't want to be the last church planted. We believe there's always room for more!

Start with this: "We're under your authority, and we're stirring on starting a church."

Next, I'll look at the clock: How long has the person been here, etc.?

Next, I'll look at the runway: How long until takeoff?

Keep the plans in a tight circle of your family and closest friends. If tons of people know about it, you will unravel the plan too much and you limit the options.

I want to be in on the process early, and I want to know the most flexible start date possible.

HERE ARE SOME GUIDELINES:

Don't do anything that confuses the body of Christ.

Try to protect the unity of this church and the churches in the area where you want to plant.

Honor the other churches in your area.

HOW WOULD YOU WANT SOMEONE TO TELL YOU THEY WANT TO LEAVE?

We aren't going to keep everyone forever. We expect a minimum of four years, we hope for ten, and we're happy with a lifetime.

In the same way people trusted us to hire them, we hope they will trust us to help them know when it's time to leave.

Not everyone will stay forever, but everyone can leave well.

HOW IMPORTANT IS IT FOR YOU TO KNOW WHERE WE SEE OURSELVES IN 5 YEARS?

A lot of churches don't like to know what people want to do in their future, but I love it!

I want to know what's in your heart. Don't lie to us about plans to leave this place. Be honest and tell the truth.

I'm mature enough to know that plans change, and God can adjust your trajectory.

Use verbiage like, "I feel God is leading me there."

Ask me how the team can make you ready for the next move, because getting ready may take two to five years.

HOW WOULD YOU WANT SOMEONE TO SHARE A CHALLENGE WITH YOU?

I want them to sidebar with me if they want to share a personal challenge with me or challenge something I'm doing at River Valley Church.

The biggest thing a leader is thinking during a challenge is: "How big is the circle?" Is this person sharing a concern, or is he or she being disloyal?

You want to show your loyalty by saying and meaning: "I love this enough to challenge it!"

It's fighting words if you say, "A lot of people have been talking…" I'll want to know who so we can root out the enemy! So don't use this phrase.

When challenging me, this is good verbiage, "This is on my heart. I don't know the whole picture, and I don't understand. Please help me."

Always go to the person you report to unless you've gone to that person enough times with little or no results. Then it's appropriate to go to the next person up the chain of authority. The person over you can't help if you skip over him or her.

IMPORTANT PRINCIPLES OF ENGAGEMENT: AGREE – SUPPORT – ALIGN

When we leave the room after a decision is made, we need everyone to support the decision. You don't have to agree with the decision. You can think, "I didn't agree with it, but I support it." It's disloyal to walk out of the meeting and tell people, "I don't like the decision." That breaks a team down.

Agreement is the hope. Support is the necessity.

Don't sabotage. You can sabotage a decision and a leader by a lack of enthusiasm, by letting people know you voted against a decision, or by not giving your full effort.

HOW SHOULD YOU RESPOND WHEN YOU MAKE MISTAKES?

Admit it when you make mistakes. I don't expect you to be perfect, but I expect you to be aware and honest.

When you make a mistake, don't give such a brief apology that people can't even feel your regret.

Tell me all the things you're ready to do to solve it! You can help your recovery by thinking of your own solutions!

Allow time for your team to feel the hurt of the mistake.

+ Admit you are wrong.

+ Let it land.

+ Move on.

Take the same approach with your team in how you handle their mistakes.

HOW I COMMUNICATE:

Emails

Bullet points and answers requiring a short response from me.

Texts

These aren't intrusive at all. I actually like this best because it's brief, it's immediate, and then it's done.

Phone Calls

Call if it's fun or you have an emergency.

In Person

I need your nonverbals to match your words. I can read your nonverbal messages better than you realize!

HOW DO I GET MORE TIME WITH YOU?

You need to get in my flight plan! Go where I'm going. Be proactive and be positive! Every leader wants to spend time with their team, but sometimes time constraints won't allow it.

MISCELLANEOUS THOUGHTS

Golf is my favorite hobby.

My wife jokes that I'm the "yes man." I usually say "yes" to anything, and those things tend to become sermon illustrations!

My love language is words of affirmation.

I hate to eat alone.

I love to travel.

I believe in giving people second chances!

ABOUT THE AUTHOR

Sam Chand's singular vision for his life is to help others succeed. A prolific author and renowned international consultant, he speaks regularly at leadership conferences, corporations, business roundtables, seminars, and other leadership development opportunities.

Being raised in a pastor's home in India has uniquely equipped Sam to share his passion to mentor, develop, and inspire leaders to break all limits. He has been called a dream releaser, leadership architect, and change strategist.

In the 1970s, as a student at Beulah Heights College, Sam served as a janitor, cook, and dishwasher to finance his education. He returned in 1989 as president—and under his leadership, Beulah Heights University became the country's largest predominantly African-American Christian college.

Sam holds an honorary Doctor of Humane Letters from Beulah Heights University, an honorary Doctor of Divinity from Heritage Bible College, a Master of Arts in Biblical Counseling from Grace Theological Seminary, and a Bachelor of Arts in Biblical Education from Beulah Heights. He has mentored leaders in churches and ministries as well as international corporations and business start-ups. He was named one of the top thirty global leadership gurus by www.leadershipgurus.net.

Sam has authored more than a dozen books on leadership, including *Culture Catalyst*, *Bigger Faster Leadership*, *Leadership Pain*, *Who's Holding Your Ladder?*, *What's Shakin' Your Ladder?*, and *12 Success Factors of an Organization*.

For more information or to connect with Sam, please visit www.sam-chand.com.

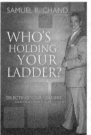

clRC
DREAM RELEASER COACHING

DREAM RELEASER COACHING

- Want to start a new career path?
- Want to help others?
- Want to increase your income from working anywhere in the world?
- Are you stuck?
- Do you want to get unstuck?

In 10 short months you could be certified with all the above through the
Dream Releaser Coaching Program.

Visit us at **www.dreamreleaser.com** to find out how to become a certified life coach.

///

DREAM RELEASER ENTERPRISE

MARKETING / DESIGN

- ☑ Marketing Funnels
- ☑ Promotional Campaign
- ☑ Landing Pages
- ☑ Copywriting
- ☑ Social Media Marketing and Management
- ☑ Branding
- ☑ Logo Design
- ☑ Business Card Design

And much more ...

BOOK PUBLISHING

- ☑ A-Z Publishing Services
- ☑ Ghost Writing
- ☑ Interior Design
- ☑ Cover Design
- ☑ Nook/Kindle/iBooks Publishing
- ☑ Distribution
- ☑ ISBN Assignments
- ☑ On-Demand & Offset Printing Options

And much more ...

WEB DEVELOPMENT

- ☑ 1 Page Website
- ☑ 5 Page Website
- ☑ Custom Website
- ☑ Blog Integration
- ☑ Shopping Cart Integration
- ☑ Database Building
- ☑ Social Media Setup
- ☑ Membership Environments

And much more ...

READY TO TAKE YOUR BUSINESS TO THE NEXT LEVEL?
Visit us at **www.dreamreleaserenterprise.com** and let us help you.

Welcome to Our House!

We Have a Special Gift for You

It is our privilege and pleasure to share in your love of Christian books. We are committed to bringing you authors and books that feed, challenge, and enrich your faith.

To show our appreciation, we invite you to sign up to receive a specially selected **Reader Appreciation Gift**, with our compliments. Just go to the Web address at the bottom of this page.

God bless you as you seek a deeper walk with Him!

WE HAVE A GIFT FOR YOU. VISIT:

whpub.me/nonfictionthx

WHITAKER
HOUSE